A WAY of LIFE

MERLON PATRICK WOODARD

Merlon Patrick Woodard - Author

A Way of Life

© 2020 by Merlon Patrick Woodard Author and Self Publishing

ISBN (Print): 978-1-09832-082-9
ISBN (eBook): 978-1-09832-083-6

FORWARD

My life has been an exciting journey. Born in the Great Depression and being raised up on a Sharecropper's farm in Johnston County, North Carolina, I can remember how poor everybody was. As time and years past me by, I can look back into those years.

Now I was a young adult. I could see my future, so I made up my mind that there was a better way of life for me. I have been cautioned not to fall into a trap where I could not get out. The more I looked back at the past, the more I stride to become somebody that I could be proud of.

In those early years I became a hard worker with a good mind to go with it. I determined that someday there would be a better life. I must not let it slip by. Now is the time to prove to myself what the future holds for me. It is what I do right that will make the difference.

In my early adult years I was still poor and had no wealth of any kind except my little house and a car. This was in the fifties and sixties. I would always talk and have several conversations with a few people that I knew were successful. Ruling out what I did not think would be beneficial to me.

My first business came about in 1969 after meeting this gentleman, a good talking person by the name of Mr. Moss, up in the center part of the state. We both were on vacation. We met each other while riding on the ferry across from the mainland Cape Carteret to Emerald Isle before the state built the bridge in 1971. He was telling me about a new business that he and his partner were starting up. He said it would not take a lot of money to do this. We talked on and I began to ask more questions because he got my attention. I was 34 years old at this time working in low class management positions. I told him what my position was with Merita Bread Company. I asked him what the business was. He said that it was the lady's hosiery business. Never would I have thought about this. I know I looked surprised. I said to him I do not know anything about the hosiery business. He said that I did not have to know anything but how to establish a route with display and sell them.

He said after talking to me that I would do good and could make a lot of money because they were just before getting popular. In my mind I started putting things together fast. We were almost across the sound. At this particular time, I was route supervisor with the Merita Bread Company in Rocky Mount, NC. It was just luck that we were together on that ferry, this family and my family at the same time.

It seems that this was the way it was throughout the rest of my life. The main thing a person has to do is be a good listener and let the other people talk if they made good sense. He said that he was from Candor, NC the peach capital of North Carolina. He went on explaining to me how good this would be and not to forget about it and call him anytime if I wanted to hear more about this.

The location that I could call on would be independent grocery stores, convenient marts, truck stops, drug stores, and on it went.

Being Route Supervisor with Merita Bread Company and having eleven truck routes out of Rocky Mount, NC, I could see where this was going. Mr. Moss said that if I decided to go forward with this that he could furnish the one size panty hose that would fit most ladies from about 100 pounds to 150 pounds. Also he said that they will have them to fit tall ladies and the big mama panty hose that will fit from about 180 to 220 pounds big ladies. He said the type of display I would use would be a swivel wire rack that was about 5 feet tall. This type of display would help the hosiery sell a lot better than any other way of displaying them. The ladies would buy them on impulse.

The panty hose in the future will replace a lot of those old single cotton hose that had to be help up with garter belts. This new type panty hose will be made out of rayon and nylon and this would be a pretty slick finish. The hosiery are made from an oil base with a synthetic fiber to give it spandex elasticity. They came in different colors, suntan, brown, coffee, black, navy, grey, and others in today markets. We are across the sound and it is time to part company. I thanked him for all this information and told him that I would certainly give it a lot of thought.

I talked to my wife about all this and she said that she was going to start wearing panty hose because they were less trouble to wear. She told me I had a good job and get my mind off this because she did not think I was suited for selling ladies hosiery. It did not leave my mind because I was tired of low class management positions. It was the money that I was thinking about not what I was selling. I thought if I could make this go that I would not have any competition.

When I was growing up on the farm as a sharecropper's son, I was my own boss and I made my own money. This I never forgot and it was burning inside of me to be what I wanted to be "to be my own boss."

I worked on with the Merita Bread Company and observed the Mom and Pop Stores throughout all the routes.

Back in the late 60's and 70"s, stores did not have any type clothes line merchandise or apparel in them. It was never thought of. People went to the clothing store to buy these products.

This gave me a good opportunity to be the first throughout all my routes. I talked to the managers and owners asking them would they let me put a hosiery display in their place.

Most said they would if they would sell, that they had never tried anything like this before. I convinced them that if they did not sell, I would remove the display and they would not owe me a cent. They all knew me and liked me. I believe this is why most of them let me in with the panty hose display. Now they are everywhere in all the stores. It did not take long before some of my locations had other dry good things in their stores after seeing how my panty hose sold.

On the days I was off, Wednesday, Saturday, and Sunday, I had to work on Sundays to get it going. I ordered my hosiery from Freeman Hosiery and my wire display racks from the Wire Product Company from Burlington, NC that would hold the panty hose. They would hold about four dozen each.

On my days off, I began to put my displays in some of the stores. It was surprising to them and me how good they sold. The retail price I put on them was .88 cents for the one size, .99 cents for the tall size, and $1.29 for the Big Mama panty hose. In about a month I had 69 locations. This was all I could work with my three days off because by then it was all I could do to replenish all I had in the stores. My salary was more now from the profit from the hosiery than Merita was paying me, I had to resign from Merita Bread Company so I could expand my business. Boy this was good I was an Entrepreneur person and becoming my own boss. I gave my two weeks' notice and they tried to raise my salary to stay. I told them I could not after the two weeks I was supposed to quit but they asked me could I stay two more weeks. I could not refuse because they had been good to me. Now this would be eight weeks from the time I began putting my displays in the stores.

Mr. Chilton wished me success and he hated to see me go. He said that he hoped that these two weeks I could train someone half as good as I was. After thirteen years, I decided to go in the Real Estate Business. I sold my business to a nice gentleman Floyd Newsome, retired from Pepsi Company out of Wilson, NC. He rode with me three weeks to learn all the locations and to understand the business.

I had approximately 200 locations traveling in all of North Carolina from Raleigh to the coast. This was a good business and Floyd knew it. He was happy because this is what suited him.

My book tells the rest of all the true stories and my adventures from when I was a little boy until now I am in my 80's.

Now you are ready to read my book and see where you could fit in!

Merlon

SYNOPSIS/SUMMARY

My early life as a Sharecropper's son was a hard life. Having been born during the Great Depression and with World War II right after, sharecroppers were about as poor as they could get.

Wealthy people were losing most of their wealth and some lost it all. Being so poor what did sharecroppers have to lose? The only way you could go with your life was to go forward. Sharecroppers were about as poor financially as they could get.

I was born on December 2, 1935. In the year 12-07-41, our President Roosevelt announced over Dad's old Philco Battery Radio that Japan had bombed Pearl Harbor. This was on Sunday morning at 7:30 a.m. He said thousands of people lost their lives and many ships were destroyed.

Scratching out a living and raising a family was hard for everyone. Living conditions and having enough to eat was a challenge. This was a way of life for most people back then with nothing to compare it to,

Mostly all farms were owned by the rich people that we called our Landlords. The main cash crops were tobacco and cotton that we sold after harvesting in the fall of the year. Two to four mules were used to farm with depending on how big your farm was. Most farms were 30 to 40 acres.

There were no tractors in the early years of the 30's and 40's in our neighborhood. Life was really slow then. I can remember when I saw my first little red Allis Chalmers tractor, I was 12 years old. It was owned by our Landlord by the name of Jim Boyett. He was a rich man, he owned about 20 farms. I was eight years old when we moved to one of his farms. This was down a wagon path about one mile from the main dirt road.

I can remember in my early life back in the 30's and 40's all roads were dirt roads or paths, except Highway 70 going north and east and 301 going north and south.

Model T Ford cars came about in the early 1900's faster than the state of North Carolina could build roads for them. Only the rich could buy them. They traveled the old dirt roads, wagon paths, and some old stagecoach roads. During the early 1900's some roads were built with plank boards. Roads after that was the dirt roads that the state built and in 1915 some paved roads came about. They were many wrecks and the car had become what they called the killing machine because the state had no stop signs. It took about 30 years before the state could catch up with the roads due to the increase of cars being sold.

As years crept by and I grew a little older, I became more adapted to my situation. Families had to raise and canned what they ate. This was the only way of having enough food year round.

Sharecroppers had hardly any money, except in the fall when they sold their crops. This took about all they had to pay out of debt to the Landlord and the Old General Store where they purchased certain things with a coupon book the General Store provided to them until they sold their corps.

Sharecroppers would help each other just like if they were their own family. They would swap labor to house their tobacco and other crops. The tobacco had to be harvested at the right time, if not it would dry up in the field. This was important. If they lost their tobacco crop they could not survive another year.

I can recall mothers having babies most of them had a midwife or a family member to help with the birth. It would be almost impossible to fetch a doctor because only about one family out of three had a car. If they could not get a doctor in time the mother or baby or both could die, a lot of them died.

My Mother lost her last baby because she could not get to the hospital in Goldsboro, NC about 30 miles away.

With the Depression coming to an end in 1939 and World War II starting in 1942, Sharecroppers got poorer than poor. Some countries were not financially wealthy enough to go to war. Mom would sell chickens, eggs, hog meat, lard, and she sold some of my rabbits that I caught in my rabbit boxes to the Mom and Pop old grocery stores.

Mom made all our clothes on an old Singer Sewing Machine that she had to pedal with her feet. Dad would put new shoe soles on our shoes. We only got new shoes when our feet would out grow the pair we were wearing.

I was six years old when I started helping around the tobacco barn. People would give me some pennies or a nickel. This was big money. Everything was cheap back in those times. I could go to the theatre and buy a Pepsi, a box of pop corn, and pay my way in the movie for 19 cents. Those pennies and nickels added up to enough to go to the movie.

My Dad never had any money to give to us kids. I was the baby. At the age of eight I made a hand at the barn. This was when I got paid 35 cents an hour to hand tobacco.

As the war went on from 1942 to 1945, the sharecroppers could hardly survive. The Government issued Ration Stamps. They came in good for a few farmers providing you had any money to buy with.

After World War II, a couple years later things began to get a little better for sharecroppers. A few months before President Roosevelt died he asked Congress to pass the G.I. Bill this enabled all the Veteran men and women that wanted to go to school of some type and college at the Government's expense. Most took advantage of this. The ones that did made a lot more money than the ones that did not. The G.I. Bill cost our Government into the billions but as years went by all this was paid back because of higher wages and more taxes was paid back to the government. This economy was getting a lot better because at the end of the forties and fifties, Manufactures and the Industrial Revolution were bringing about thousands of jobs. This was one of the fastest growths in our country's history.

At the age of 13, I began to catch muskrats. The fur business was good at this time. I could sell a muskrat hide for $1.75, this was more than I could make when farming.

At the age of 16 years old, we moved to another farm near the town of Selma with Dad's old 1937 Chevrolet Coupe. I found a job part time on Friday evening and all day on Saturday with Vernon Wigg's Supermarket. This was a better store than the Mom and Pop's Grocery Stores.

I saved every cent I could because I needed a car. If I did not work my car out I would not get one. There is a lot I am leaving out in my book. By barning tobacco and helping everybody I could, I bought 17 pigs at weaning age from the sow to go in my soybean field. I got a school bus to drive in the 11th and 12th grades. With my $22.00 a month, my pigs, and working with Mr. Wiggs, I bought me a car before I started back in the 12th grade.

While driving a school bus in the 11th grade in 1954, Hurricane Hazel came through and I was on my bus route when this happened.

My book breaks it down in detail how poor we were. The Landlord's houses were poor construction with no running water, electric, and no inside plumbing. We used little lantern lamps with oil. Our furniture was home made. The women in the neighborhood helped each other quit quits and we had feather beds for our mattress.

My book breaks it down and explains everything in detail how I started my businesses and what motivated me to start these particular businesses. After a few years I would sell my business and start another.

When I was in Florida in my Commercial Fishing Business, I witnessed the space ship Challenger coming over the horizon one morning just before I put my boat in Indian River at the boat landing. This was a big area for boats and trucks. There were lots of people to watch the flight that morning when it blew up.

A few years after finishing high school and being employed with three big retail giants about 14 years all total, adding to my experiences with them to what I know I decided it was time to be self-employed. I dreamed of being my own boss for so long and now is the time to become my own Entrepreneurship person and after all my Entrepreneur Businesses. My last business was my Hot Dog Cart Business on the Camp Lejeune Marine Corps Base during the years 2016 to 2018.

Ancestry:

My Mother's ancestry DNA came from around the globe. Her DNA is divided among four categories which are English, Whale, Iceland, and East Africa people.

Mom's DNA came from four different native tribes in four different small province regions joining each other in East Africa. They were the Benin, Togo, Cameroon, and Bantu Tribes. Her DNA mixed with these four regions.

My book tells the stories about Mom's African people. Also my book tells about the Civil War, my grandfather during this time in history, and my Great-grandfather having been born a slave on a plantation in Duplin County, NC.

He married the plantation owner's daughter both having been born the same year in 1805. How they became husband and wife. My grandfather, William Billy Carter was born in the year 1837 and died in 1929 and about his marriage to my grandmother Lara Bedford Carter. There is a lot to tell!!

The book mentions Michael Rockerfellow the son of Nelson Rockerfellow when he went to explore the New Genua Native Jungle and how the natives killed him and ate his body!

My mother had many ancestries. These are mentioned in my book, their marriages to whom and about their lives.

I hope this book will inspire the younger generation that nothing is free. You have to make your own way. You have to decide what you want out of life and which way you want to go to become somebody or to be a dead beat all your life.

Nobody will ever hand you anything. If you are not careful the dishonest people will swindle you out of everything you have.

The way life is now you have to be smart and with good common sense to know the difference. Yes you can be somebody, but it is all entirely up to you. You do not have to be really smart it also takes a little common sense with it. The hard working people are the ones that have made our nation what it is today. You have to count your blessings everyday what God has given you in all of your life. It is all in your hands now and with God's help you can have your dreams and contribute a lot to society. You must follow your dreams and don't be a quitter. Yes you can do it. Don't let it be impossible, stay focused and make your life a successful one. Let's make things become reality. In the end at an old age you will look back on your life and thank God that I am somebody and I fought a big fight, I won, and I accomplished my dreams.

A Way of Life

By

Merlon Patrick Woodard

I was a Sharecropper's Son born on a little farm near Boon Hill (Princeton) North Carolina, in Johnston County. This was during the Great Depression. People were losing most of their wealth and some rich people lost it all. But being so poor, what did you have to lose? The only way was to go forward because most Sharecroppers were about as poor financially as they could get.

Scratching out a living and raising a family was hard for everyone. Living conditions and having enough to eat was a challenge. This was a way of life, with nothing to compare it too.

As years crept by and I grew older, a little at a time, I became more adapted to my situation. Families had to raise and canned what they ate or starve. People did not have much money. Sharecroppers would help each other to survive.

During these times in my early life medical help and doctors were out of the question. Many people died young, especially mothers having babies, mostly at child birth.

Everything was at a slow pace back then, with the Depression coming to an end in 1939. World War II started in 1941. Some countries were not financially wealthy enough to go to war.

I grew up with good common sense and a little smarts to go with it. Making the best of what I could do on just the little that I had at a young age.

Going to school was not easy and working on the farm at a young age starting at about 6 years old until I finished High School, a lot of school children did not finish.

As the war went on, Sharecroppers could hardly survive. The government issued Ration Stamps for all the people. They came in good at times, providing you had any money to buy anything with.

For years I wanted to tell my true stories about my past. Many of my friends encouraged me to write a book. Back in the early 1900's, it was hard for people to survive with neighbors helping neighbors as if they were your own family was really important.

The conditions that most sharecroppers lived in were almost unbelievable and unbearable. This was a way of life for all for many years to come.

With poor housing, no electric, no running water, no inside plumbing, and with no insulation in some of the rooms. My Mother would buy this cheap linoleum. This would keep most of the wind out.

Things got a little better a few years after the war. I began to grow up and had a good mind about myself. Before I finished High School, I was making my own living. I became an Entrepreneur the rest of my life. I contributed a lot to our society throughout my life. With my businesses, I have helped create hundreds of jobs.

This book will hopefully help young people find their way in life and their future. Remember you have to make your own future the same as the author did.

My name is Merlon Patrick Woodard. For several years I have wanted to tell my part of history, growing up on a farm. I was born in the year December 2, 1935 during the end of the Depression in the state of North Carolina in Johnston County. They were hard times, after the Depression only about one family out of three had a Model T Ford or a car of any kind.

I can remember when I was four years old, I am in my 80's now. The first thing I can remember is when my Mom took our picture with an old Kodak Camera, I was four years old then. There were four children in the family, (L.B.) Lenwood Ballard, Roy McCray, and my sister Laura Ellen, I was the youngest. My father was Ballard Woodard and my mother was Nancy Carter Woodard. We lived on a farm and we were Sharecroppers. Giving half of what we made to our landlord. I lived the next 20 years in Johnston County, NC. The first place that I can remember we lived up on a hill and the front of the yard was a steep hill. It sloped down to the road. I learned how to ride my dad's old bicycle down the hill, after falling off a few times it got easier to ride!! I would put my right leg through the bicycle bars and push off with my left foot and down I went, I was too little to paddle it. The hill sloped just right so the bicycle would slow down and stop on its own.

I can remember a big snow storm we had that year it was 1940. Roy and Laura were waiting for the school bus when the snow started falling, by the time the bus came back that evening there was a lot of snow on the ground. Dad went down the hill to help Roy and Laura up the hill to the house. He put one under each arm and brought them up the hill. Roy was in the second grade and Laura was in first. They were 13 months apart. L.B. being the oldest was seven, he did not go to school because he was handicapped. Back then the state did not have a special school that he could attend.

That was a cold winter on December 2, 1940. I turned five years old. We moved that winter by mule and wagon about five miles from where we were living. When summer came it was my first year going blueberry picking. Just about all the families did this. We looked for them in the woods. They were easy to find.

We lived down a path with woods all around us. The blueberry bushes were average size and most of the time you could reach the top. They were not tall just big around. Some bushes had blueberries as big as your thumb. Everyone picking had a bucket. After the day was over we would put all the blueberries in a bushel basket and most of the time we would almost fill the basket full. My mother could make the best blueberry pie in the whole world. Without a refrigerator to keep them cold, they would only last a few days, needless to say all we kids got a belly full of pie!

Back in the early years, sharecroppers had no money. Living on a farm was a poor way to live. Most people living on a farm back then didn't know any better because that was the way everyone lived! We were Sharecroppers. There were no tractors, all the work on the farm was done with two or three mules.

On December 2, 1941, I turned six years old and on December 7, 1941, Dad was listening to the battery operated radio on Sunday around 7:30 a.m. Dad heard President Roosevelt announce that Japan had attacked Pearl Harbor and took thousands of lives and lots ships were destroyed! There were many families that lived on the dirt road. Our closest neighbor was a black gentleman and he came over to the house shortly after the bombing of Pearl Harbor, not knowing what had happened. His name was Dee Troublefield, a good neighbor that would help you do anything. Dad asked him if he had heard the radio this morning. He told Dad his battery was dead in his radio and he did not have any money to buy a new battery. A new battery would cost as much as a radio would cost. The battery was dry cells and they could not be charged! Nobody had electric anyway. Dad said to Dee, "them damn old Japs attacked Pearl Harbor this morning and thousands of people were killed and a lot of ships were destroyed!" They talked on about the attack and said the President stated we will have to get ready for war! I got scared and while they were talking, a child did not interrupt! Children did not speak until they were spoken to. I looked up to Dad and pulled his britches leg overalls, which I have done many times before, he looked down at

me and asked me what do you want boy? I said to him what is a Jap? He told me it was people from another country trying to kill us! I was really scared and ran to Mom and told her what Dad told me and she said to me that the Japs were a long ways off in another country and they would not harm us.

Moving to Another Farm:

We moved that Christmas week to another farm that had a better house to live in. We used two mules and a wagon to move our furniture and everything else we had. The mules moved the farm equipment to our new house, which was four miles away. The house we moved in was a big yellow house fronting the Atlantic coastline. The railroad track, a short distance down the path from 301 Hwy that went North to South from New York to Florida! The path was a short path from the old 301! The house was about 300 feet from the road. Beside the path down a little ways toward the old 301 was a well that we got our water. It was under a big oak tree near the Hwy. We lived on the outskirts of a little town called Micro. They had a school from first to twelfth grade. That year in the fall when school started back, I was almost seven. I can remember Dad farming, hitching up the mule and my brother Roy was big enough to help a little. I can remember those old steam engine choo-choo trains coming down the railroad tracks. It sounded like they were coming through the house!

The well where we got our water was a big well! There was a board across the top of the well with a wheel, so you could let the rope with a bucket attached, to pull the water out of the well. We built a shelf beside the well to hold the bucket when you pulled it out of the well. It made pouring from one bucket to another easier. That big oak tree shaded the well and I believe it kept the water cold! Everybody loved our water from that well!

Getting Ready For The War

That same year in 1942, the U.S. was getting ready for war with Japan. The main source of travel was 301 Hwy from North to South. The army convoy would stop about every other day to get water from our well. They could see our well from the Hwy, it was a convenient place to pull off the road and fill up all their canteens and buckets. They also filled up their Jeeps and trucks. I believe the word got out where they could find water along the route they were traveling. They could not miss that big old yellow house and well. In our neighborhood electric and running water came about in the late 40's early 50's! The military got their water that year and the years after that. I wish I had a dollar for each bucket of water that came out of that well! All the share-cropper families had outside toilets or out houses. A lot of the army boys would use our out houses during these years. We had no toilet paper, we mostly used newspaper or Sears Roebuck Catalogues and corn cobs!

Making Soap:

Families back in the early years made their own soap. We used soap to take a bath, wash our hands, and wash clothes with. We did not have access to anything like wash powders or fancy soap!

We had two big wash pots for boiling and washing clothes. Mom would make lye soap in the small pot! When she made the soap it would last a long time. This is how Mom made the soap. She put some side meat from the hog in the pot and heat the pot with wood to melt the grease out of the fat meat and then mix the lye in the pot with the fat. After the lye dissolved she would add water and boil for a short time. If there were any meat or bones, she would remove them. She would next add pine needles to the pot for a short time, and then remove them. This would give it a little bit of pine smell! She would remove the wood from around the pot so it could cool. She would stir the pot for about ten minutes and then let it cool and harden in the pot. After it hardened she would cut it in small squares and let it set for two to four weeks.

To wash clothes she would heat both big pots with the right size pieces of wood to fit the pots. When the water got hot, she would put light colored clothes in one and dark and heavy clothes in the other along with lye soap. She would boil about twenty minutes, along while at times, punching the clothes with a stick that was round at the bottom so it would not tear the clothes! She had a scrub board that she used to clean the clothes.

She still had to draw more water from the well to rinse the clothes, so I had a bucket that I helped fill her wash pots again for rinsing. This was a job! She would rinse and then she would squeeze the water out of each piece and then hang them on the clothes line to dry. When the clothes dried, she would fold and put some away and some she had to iron, using the wood stove and cast iron. She had two irons that she alternated to the wood stove to get hot! It was an all day job to wash clothes. Mom did this about once a week, summer and winter. Laura would help Mom when she got big enough.

We had a pot belly stove that used coal or wood in the living room, in the front of the house, and in the kitchen. We had a wood burning cook stove, for the winter months this was good, but in the summer it was hot. Mom would open up all the doors and windows. During these years most farm families would not have any screens in the windows. Mom could only cook what we could eat. The things like potatoes and vegetables would keep until we could eat them.

The years we lived near the railroad tracks, hobos would walk the tracks and beg for food. They would stop during the day and anything Mom could spare, she would give it to them and give them water most of the time. Most of the time there would only be one of them. Mom knew they would come by just about every other day. She would try to keep some baked sweet potatoes and biscuits and maybe a piece of side meat that we did not eat that morning.

Back in the 40's people were poor about the only way farmers had to travel was with mules and wagons or a buggy, only a few people had a Model T Ford. The Model T Ford did not have a starter, but some had lights. No turn signal, you would hold your arm out the window in an up hand position to turn right and straight out for a left turn and down beside the door to slow down or stop. The Model T Ford used a crank to crank it. This was a metal piece of iron that made an elbow with the end part that went in the engine to turn the fly wheel. It took two or three good turns to get it started. The Model T had good brakes, some had gas pedals and some did not. Early models had levers on the steering column to slow down or go faster.

Living poor back before the 50's, you did not know how poor you were because you had nothing to compare it to! Every family lived poor and the whole family had to pull together to get things done. People had big families in the early years, the bigger the better to be able to help with the farming. Families pulling together and helping each other was a must and when someone got sick the other families in the neighborhood all pulled together to help you. I remember one year this farmer got sick and almost died and the whole neighborhood pitched in and housed his tobacco for him. The tobacco crop was most important because the tobacco could not wait in the fields to be harvested because if left too long it would dry up. It had to be harvested once a week until it was finished.

Staying Warm in the Winter:

We would saw and chop wood during the fall for our wood burning stoves, one in the living room and one in the kitchen. We also walked up and down the railroad tracks in front of our big yellow house picking up coal that would fall off the train when it passed by. The coal would last longer than wood. We found a lot of coal.

It was just as hard staying warm in the winter as it was staying cool in the summer. Sometimes the iron stove in the living room would wear out and if we did not have the money to buy another, we would use the fireplace. The fireplace did not give out as much heat and spread it throughout the rooms like the wood heater.

When we all went to bed, we slept on a feather bed mattress and box springs for the bottom. Some mornings when we got out of bed water would be frozen in the house.

Without bathrooms, at night we would use slop jars instead of going outside to use the privy! Sometimes it was so cold the urine would freeze in the bedroom slop jars! But that old feather bed would keep us warm. Mom would get up first and get the fire going in the stove and the cook stove. When we kids got up in the morning, we would get our clothes together and dance around the stove while putting them on, after a while you would get warm.

Homemade clothes:

Mom had this old Singer sewing machine that she used to make most of our clothes. When we were little, we had no money to buy anything. We just had to make do with what we had. The sewing machine was in a cabinet with four legs and it had a drawer underneath it, a foot pedal that you made go up and down at the speed you wanted. There was a spool of thread that went over the spindle on the top of the sewing machine and she would thread through the bobbin and down to the needle. This machine did a good job sewing just about anything and did a lot of patch work on overalls! Mom made all of our overalls for my two brothers and me. She would buy denim material by the yard and she was good at this. She had patterns to make anything we wore. I was 12 years old before I had my first store bought overalls! Mom would make Laura's dresses from the material she bought at the general store. We bought our flour in 100 pound sacks that Mom would use to make Laura's dresses also. These sacks were pretty. They had flowers on them with different designs! It was just as pretty as the cloth mom would buy by the yard at the general store.

Mom worked all the time, winter and summer, keeping the house clean, cooking, farm work, taking care of the chickens, and hatching out biddies. If your shoe bottom wore out we had what you called a shoe mold. Dad would fix our shoes on the mold. The mold would go down inside the shoe then turn the shoe upside down and nail tacks in the shoe bottom. The shoe mold was metal and when he nailed the tacks in and through the new shoe bottom, the tacks would not come through the shoe. After that he would put a new heel on the shoe! Then he would trim the bottom to fit the shoe. We did not have money to buy new shoes. We only got new shoes when the shoes we had would get too small for us (our feet).

Bathing:

Mom heated the water that she drew out of the well in a big bucket on the cook stove. We used the wash tub to bathe in. She would pour the hot water in and then add cold water to get the right temperature. We would all take turns getting in the tub one at a time. We all had to use the same water with lye soap. We were poor and the house we lived in would not meet the standards of today, but Mom made sure we had a clean house and clean clothes.

We boys wore overalls with holes in the knees from playing marbles and working on the farm. Now this generation of today is a different story. They want to pay up to $200.00 for shoes and jeans! During these years just about all of the boys and some girls would play marbles at school. This is how it was done, you would take your shoe hill of your foot and draw a circle in the hard dirt (ground). Each person would start with five marbles and a special marble (our favorite) that you called a "steelie". You would have two to four players shooting marbles. To start the game off we put all the players' marbles in the middle of the circle. Everyone would take their turn and the one who got the most marbles out would win the game. That person would go first the next game.

Each pack of marbles you bought would have what they called a "log cart". It was bigger than the rest of the marbles. It was suppose to be used to break the marbles in the center. We soon found out it was better to use a "steelie", a steel ball. You got more marbles out of the ring! So we used the little steel balls that came from a machine shop. Boy, when you hit the marbles just right it would really break up the marbles in the ring. The person shooting would keep on until he didn't shoot a marble out the ring and then it was the next person's turn. We kids would walk around all day at school with marbles in our pockets.

First Ice Cream Cone:

On a hot fall day, Dad took the whole family to town, we all road in the wagon pulled by one mule. Dad had come from selling tobacco the day before. This is the first time I could remember going to town. I was about four years old, Laura was six, brother Roy was 7, and LB was 9. Mom and Dad sat on the seat across the front of the wagon. Selma was not far away, so it did not take that long to get there that Saturday. Everybody went to town on Saturday. I can't remember what all we bought, but I can remember one thing in particular I had never seen before! It was a cone of ice cream! I knew what ice cream was because we had made ice cream before with a neighbor. LB, Roy, and Laura knew what it was, but this was new to me! I ate the ice cream and made sure I got it all with my fingers down in the cone. Then I threw the cone on the ground. Roy and Laura saw what I did and they told Mom and Dad. Mom asked me "why did I throw the cone away"? I told her it was wood and didn't want to eat it! Everybody had a good laugh over that! But it never happened again!

We lived out in the country and the school was about a ½ mile away from where we lived. We went to micro school. We had to walk by following the train tracks to the school house. It had grades first through the twelfth in one small building. Students had to carry their lunch back then. We had no lunch room. Most of the time we ate breakfast and did not have anything left to take for lunch. When we came home from school we would get our dinner. We ate two meals a day unless we ate some table scraps before we went to bed. We had food to eat such as it was, but nothing fancy. It was a long time before I saw loaf bread. Mom would make biscuits! Sometime we had a nickel or dime and when we went to school we would stop at Mom & Pop Store and Roy would buy us an apple or orange! This did not happen very often. We would get fruit at Christmas time. We just did not have all these things year around.

Farm House:

Most farm houses were made cheap and did not have insulation of any kind. Some of the rooms were not finished with sheet rock. I never saw any carpet or linoleum in any of them. Some of the floors had holes in the floors and the Landlord did not keep them up. We would move in right behind another family all the houses were on blocks and you could see all under the house. Lots of times, we would have to spray the whole house with DDT to get rid of the bed bugs (chinchs) and flies. No window screens. We had to put our own screens in the windows. The doors had no locks, only a wooded door with latch that would fall into a slot. In the winter we could not keep the cold air out! It was hard to stay warm in winter.

If you were lucky, you would have an old hand pump. By priming it with water, it would pump the water and when it gave out of water you had to go to the general store and by a seal so it would not lose its prime! To make this possible, you had to run iron pipe from the well (if the well was not too far from the house, we would build a shelf on the back porch where the pump was to be located. This made it much more convenient to pump water. On the shelf we put a wash basin and some of Mom's homemade lye soap and hang a towel on a nail. The house did not have any type of skirting around the bottom of the house!

Making Quilts:

During the winter the women folks would get together and have quilting parties! They would use any type of material they could find. They sewed squares of material together until they had the size quilt they needed. It required two pieces of material the same size to finish the quilt. They put some kind of insulation on the inside to make it warmer. Mom and Dad would make a frame big enough to stretch the material out tight and attach it to the frame. Mom would take gin cotton and put it between the top and bottom layer real thin. She would then take the top layer of the material and lay it down on the cotton. This would create insulation between the quilt. There would be from four to six women sewing a section at a time with needles moving from the top through the material and then up from the bottom making small stitches as they sewed the bottom making small stitch as they sewed the top and bottom together. They would work from the inside inward toward the outside the last thing they did was to sew all four sides together pulling the thread tight. This way the quilt would not unravel.

Bed Frame:

The bed frame would be made out of boards with a head board and foot board with four legs and four slats across the bottom to support the box springs. The mattress would be made from feathers and goose feathers! The mattress would be thick and when Mom would fluff it up it would have a lot of air in it. When you went to bed at night the bed was soft and our body would sink down in it. It was soft and warm! We had feather pillows too. They were the best pillows I ever slept on! About all the furniture we had in the house was home made by a local carpenter. During the early years we had to do the best we could! No one had money to buy new things. The only time we had money was when the crops were sold!!

Garden and Canning:

Growing a garden and canning was the only way we had to preserve our food for days and months. We did not even have a refrigerator! In the early 1900's it was hard to keep food on the table, especially if you had a big family! Everybody had to work on the farm to make it work. We only had money when we sold our crops, the rest of the year we had no money. We grew beans, peas, corn, okra, potatoes, squash, tomatoes, cabbage, collards, turnips, watermelon, and cantaloupes. Mom had a big metal canner that would hold six quart jars at a time. It had a temperature gauge on top of the lid. Everything had to cook a certain temperature. It was a slow process and hard work. She would put a teaspoon of salt in each jar and then she would screw the tops on, real loose until they cooled down and then she would tighten the lids. She would give the jars a little shake to mix the salt up and then she would put the jars in the pantry to be used as we needed.

The first big supermarket I can remember was the "Great Atlantic and Pacific Tea Company" better known as "A & P". It was a must to have a garden and can our vegetables if you wanted anything to eat during the winter. Mom would keep a low fire going in the cook stove, so our canned food would not freeze. The A & P Super Markets were located in big towns, but most Sharecroppers had no money anyway. Mom would let the fire in the heater die down at night by closing up the damper so it would not burn fast. The next morning Mom would get up and make the fire. There would still be hot coals in the stove so Mom would add lite wood and it would start burning faster and then she would add wood!

At night you did not want to go outside to the "privy", so we had a slop jar that we used. This was a white bucket with a lid. It would be so cold at night that the potty would freeze. We were nice and warm laying on the feather bed mattress! The next morning Mom would take and empty and clean the slop jar. The kids grabbed their clothes and ran to the pot belly stove to stay warm while they got dressed.

While we got ready for school Mom was in the kitchen, getting our breakfast ready. The kitchen and the living room were the only two rooms that had an oil lamp and heat! My Mom was a good cook. She would make buttermilk biscuits that were so good, they would melt in your mouth! Most of the time for breakfast, we had country ham, scrambled eggs, grits, and biscuits with butter and black strap molasses. We had coffee to drink. We would soak our biscuits in the sweet coffee and mix the red eye gravy with the molasses on the biscuit. If we had biscuits left, we would take them to school with us. Mom used a lot of flour. We had this long wooden bowl that Mom made her biscuits in. If we had some pork cracklings left, she would mix some in the biscuits. This made the biscuits even better, especially with the molasses and red eye gravy.

Babies Born at Home:

During the early years of the 1900's and before, mothers had their babies at home. Most of the mothers had a midwife to stay with them when they were in labor. Sometimes a doctor would deliver the baby! A family member would be there to help with the chores for a few days. Most mothers nursed their babies unless they had a problem! Sometimes they would use cow's milk since most of the families had a cow.

There were a lot of mothers and babies that did not make it back then, sometime the doctor did not arrive on time. Sometime the cord was wrapped around the baby's neck. There was so much that could go wrong! Keep in mind everything was slow moving back then. A lot of people still used horses to travel. If you were lucky enough to have a Model T Ford it did not go very fast with dirt roads.

My Mother and Father were married in April 21, 1929. Mom was nineteen and Dad was twenty-six. They had a family of four living children and two that died at birth.

With mom's first child LB, my Mother became ill during her pregnancy and the doctor told my Dad it was colitis and it would be bad for the baby. The disease is bowel inflammation and it attacked the immune system. It made the pregnancy very difficult, but the baby did live! When my Mom was in her fourth month of pregnancy the doctor told my Dad that she could die if she went through with the pregnancy. The doctor told Dad to make a decision about ending the pregnancy and he decided to end it because Mom was in so much pain! They gave Mom something to help end the pregnancy and waited for her to have a miscarriage. What they gave her did not work and she ended up having the baby. Mom was only twenty-one years of age at this time. It was really bad on Mom's health and she was in the bed for most of the pregnancy. They did not expect the baby to live and it was a surprise that he did and he lived to be sixth-seven years old!! The doctor did check on Mom and the baby, but there wasn't much he could do for the stomach pain. The medication he gave her to lose the baby caused the baby to be a special needs child. They did not expect him to live above childhood but he did! LB was born during Mom's seventh month and only weighed two and one half pounds. He died March 5, 1997.

The second child was a girl named Dorthy, she lived 10 days after birth. Mom's last baby was a baby boy. He was too big at birth and died. My Mom was a small woman about 5 feet tall and she had a small frame so the doctor said it would be hard for her to deliver a big baby!

My other brother Roy was born November 19, 1932, without complications, then my sister Laura Ellen was born December 3, 1933 with no complications. My brother Roy died September 12, 1992 with colon cancer. My sister Laura is still living.

My Mom was born February 6, 1910 and she died March 21, 1969 at the age of 59. My Dad was born April 9, 1903 and died December 11, 1983 at the age of 80. My brother L.B. outlived Roy and Mom!

Mom's Last Baby:

My Mom had all of us at home. Not too many people went to the hospital. My Mom only stood 5 feet tall and when she was ready to deliver her baby, Dad would try to get word to the doctor in time for them to come to the house, no one in the neighborhood had a phone so we had to do the best we could. The little town of Princeton was about five miles away and Dad had his close neighbor to get the doctor because Dad could not leave the family. Mom was in labor by the time the doctor got there. The doctor examined my Mom and told Dad this is going to be bad. He could not save my Mom and the baby! The baby weighed about 10 pounds. Dad asked the doctor, "what would you do if it was your wife" and the doctor said I would save your wife because you have four children to take care of and they are going to need their mother. He would do what he could and see what happens. He put my Mom to sleep and found out the baby was too big and so he had to cut the baby out of Mom!

There was a lot of blood from the surgery and they heard my baby brother cry out a couple of times and then he died. The doctor had to kill the baby to save my Mom's life! Mom laid there unconscious and the doctor did all he could to keep Mom alive. He told my Aunt Sally and Dad what to do for her and he would be back the next day. Mom was in and out of consciousness and Aunt Sally kept her warm and did what she could to keep her comfortable. The doctor did come back the next day and he told Dad he did not expect her to live through the night The doctor gave Mom medication and told my Aunt to try to feed her. Mom laid around a long time, she was so weak she could hardly even walk. My Aunt prayed for her every day and I do believe God heard her! Thank God Mom did not die and leave four babies. I have never heard of any mother going through what my Mom did with all of her sickness and did not die. We were very lucky!

About L.B.:

L.B. was the first child born, February 16, 1930. He lived with us as long as my Mom was able to take care of him. He was a good boy. I remember him being my big brother. He was very playful. We always played together and at an early age I knew L.B. was different. L.B. loved Mom and he was what we called a "moma's boy". My Mom spoiled him because of his condition. He could do a few things on his own, but most of the time you had to help him. He always had someone to be with him. He learned to talk when he was three or four years old. He would say short sentences, but could not put sentences together. All the kids played together and were all good to L.B.

Years passed as we grew older and big enough to work on the farm, we always took L.B. along with us and he would play with the small children, even though he was much larger! He was very pleasant, never violent, so he was a pleasure to be around. He learned to go to the bathroom and put on his clothes (with a little help). He always had to have someone keep an eye on him and help him if he needed help. After all the sickness Mom had she was still a great Mom to all the kids. As L.B. grew older and bigger it got to the place that Mom could not take care of him. L.B. was sixteen at the time that Mom and Dad decided to put L.B. in a special school. Mom's health was failing and she just could not take care of him anymore. His school was in Goldsboro at the O'Berry Center. It was in 1946 that he went to live at the Center. He was in a good section with boys near his own age. It was a nice place, he had his own bed and a chest for his clothes with three meals a day and nice people to take care of him. This was a state institution supported by the state and did not cost the family anything.

By this time Dad had bought a Model T Ford and it was not far to travel to see L.B. We all had to work hard in the fields and we thought L.B. had it better than we did. We would bring him home four times a year to stay with us for about a week at a time. He did adjust well to his new home.

L.B. enjoyed his radio and we always took him new batteries when we visited. He always wanted to go to the convenient store to get a hot dog and a Pepsi Cola!

When L.B. stayed in the O'Berry Center some of the nurses would tell us people put their loved ones in here and then forgot about them, but we did not do this. We visited L.B. as often as we could and we would take him to the Woodard Reunion when we could.

L.B. was diagnosed with cancer of the spleen and he lived about a year after the doctor found the cancer. He went to live in a nursing home so he would have better care. He was a good brother and he never hurt anyone or caused any problems. I thank God for my brother L.B.! After L.B. passed away I have never stopped thinking about him. We all should be blessed that we are born in good health.

The Old General Store:

From a mule collar to molasses, we could buy anything from the old general store. Dad bought clothes for us and material for Mom to make clothes that we could not afford to buy from the general store. We could buy canned goods, salted meats, bedding material, sheets, and things for the bed, rice, peas, all types of dry foods to eat. We took our gallon jug to put the molasses in we drew it out of a fifty gallon barrel. Most of the time, Dad would buy a hundred pounds of flour. Not only did we eat a lot of biscuits, but Mom made dumplings and pies! The flour bag was big enough to make my sister dresses. It would take two bags to make a dress. With six people in the family it did not take long to use a hundred pound bag of flour. My Mom made the best biscuits I have ever eaten!

We had a cow for several years. The cow would have a calf every two years so she would continue on giving milk. Keep in mind we had no way to keep milk, we had no electricity.

The well-to-do-people had an ice box. It was about five feet high and thirty inches wide and eighteen inches deep! The top was made to hold a big block of ice. It had a tube inside running down to the floor for melting water. A big block of ice that was bought from town was only ten cents. It took about six days for it to melt! The milk would keep about six or seven days with the ice. Everyone had a big family back in the early days.

The ice box cost about thirty dollars if you could afford it. Mom had a churn that she would use for making butter and butter milk. The churn was a round container and at the top it has a lid with a hole in it, that was where the hand pole would fit into. She would churn the milk up and down with short strokes until she could see the butter start to form on the churn stick. She would then take the butter from the churn and mold it into small squares to use at the table and for cooking. By us not having an ice box, Mom would take a quilt and wrap the milk and butter in it and put it next to the block of ice Dad made a wooden box with a lid on it where we kept the ice and milk and drinks. Mom kept the ice box under the house in the shade away from the sun. From time to time we had to buy another block of ice. I was fourteen years old before we had electricity in the house and then we only had two light bulbs because the power coming into the house was not strong enough for anything else.

Raising Chickens:

Mom would raise and grow her biddies mostly in the summer so the young chicks could survive. They had a better chance to grow. She would have about five to ten hens sitting on about twelve eggs. The color of the chicken feathers determined the color of the eggs. Our eggs were mostly white to light brown and sometimes dark brown. It would take about twenty-one to twenty-two days for the biddies to hatch from the eggs. All the hens would not hatch at the same time. This was good, so mom would have less work to do feeding them. When they came out of the nest, they would follow the mommy hen around near the barn yard. Mom would feed the biddies with crumbled up cold biscuits for a few days, then she would give them biddie feed for about two weeks, and after that they ate shelled corn like the other chickens. We had a hand turned corn sheller and it would shell a bushel basket of corn in a short time. We fed the chickens each day by just throwing and scattering the corn in the barn yard The chickens were not pinned up they could go about as they pleased. We had a chicken house where they could roost and lay their eggs. Mom had several hen's nest in the hen house and we would gather lots of eggs each day. We had about fifty chickens at all times and we ate a lot of fried chicken. We had to watch out for the hawks, they would catch our little biddies if we did not protect them! We had scare crows up around the barn to scare off the hawks, even then they would catch a lot of our biddies. Believe it or not, the crows would catch them right after they were hatched.

During the early years most of the farmers had guineas and they would roam from one farm to another, at night they would come back to their original location where they belonged. They would lay their eggs anywhere. They went about their business similar to quail. There were lots of them, so if you wanted to kill one to eat, we did so. That is just about the way it was. It was very hard to find the guineas' nests you had to watch them carefully and sometimes you would see it go to a ditch bank where they would have plenty of grass and weeds to camouflage their nest. It was easy to find if you knew what to look for. They would cover the nest after laying their eggs and then uncover the nest to lay eggs. Sometimes you would find a guinea's nest with fifteen to twenty eggs at a time. They would travel in flocks similar to wild turkeys. They would make a funny little noise after leaving their nest, so we knew then that was the nest. The eggs are a little smaller than an average chicken egg, it would be round and brown with speckles spots on them.

One reason people had a lot of guineas was because they helped protect the crops from insects, worms, caterpillars, and ants. They would also eat tobacco worms from the plants. They would help your garden by eating the insects so they served a good purpose

If Mom needed cash she would take live chickens to the general store and sell them. She did not get very much money, but sometimes she had no choice. We were very poor!

When Mom wanted chicken for dinner she would build a fire around the wash pot and get the water hot so that she could dip the chicken in the hot water so the feathers would come off easy. To catch the chicken to cook she had a long rod with a hook at the end so she could catch the chicken by the leg with the hook. Whichever chicken she wanted she would slip up on it and grab that leg with the hook. She would wring the chicken's neck, make sure it was dead, then put it in hot water, and pluck the feathers. Mom could make the best chicken and dumplings that you have ever eaten!

Hog Killing:

Dad would keep two sows just about all the time. He also had a prize boar for breeding. If we had too many hogs for what we needed, Dad would sale them. He would always keep the best looking ones for hog killing. It would take three months (3 months, 3 weeks, and 3 days – 114 days) for the sow to give birth to a liter of ten pigs (on average). He would keep the pigs in a small pen with a lot of wheat straw for bedding. The bedding would be essential for the winter months.

When the pigs got six weeks old Dad would remove the sow from them for weaning. He would put the sow in the pasture with the other hogs. By this time the pigs would be eating good. Dad gave them ground up hog feed for about two more weeks. Then he would put them in the pasture. In October he would take four or five and put them in a small pen with a floor. The purpose of this was so the hogs he would slaughter for the family to eat would be clean and free of worms. In the small pen they could not move around like in the pasture and they would gain more weight and have more fat on them. This is important because the meat would be more tender and fatter. They would have more lard that Mom used to cook with.

Dad would kill our hogs around Christmas time depending on how cold the weather was. He would wait for a cold snap just before Christmas or a few days after depending on the weather. We had to have three or four days of thirty to forty degree temperatures so the meat would not spoil before it took the salt. After three of four days the meat was safe to eat. At the end of two weeks, Dad would remove the dry salt from the meat or it would get too salty. He would then hang it up in the smoke house to let it air! The rats and mice could not get to it. If it remains laying down, the rodents would eat holes in the meat. Most of the time neighbors would help us kill hogs and we would help them. There would be no money passed, just neighbors helping neighbors.

Dad would make sure we had things in place come hog killing time. Things that would be needed: water, vat, tables, benches, hanging rack to hang the hog, pots, pans, tubs, sharp knives, buckets, chairs, split wood, salt and lots of hot water! First the water vat needed to be hot for scalding the hog. This is the way we used the vat; we laid the vat over a ten foot trench (about two feet wide and eighteen inches deep) this would look like a small ditch. All around the bottom of the vat on all four sides we put dirt. This would not let the smoke out. At one end we had cut wood and at the other end we had a flu pipe about six feet high for it to draw the fire and smoke under the vat and out the smoke stack. Dad would fill the vat with about eighteen inches of water. He would get the fire going to heat the water. Year after year we would use the same trench and do other things about the same way each year. It would take a long time pumping or drawing water from the well, keep in mind we had no running water because we had no electricity.

The vat was made out of tin or aluminum. The vat was constructed with 2 x 4's at the bottom and top corners and from side to side. It would have a 2 x 4 the width of the vat laid on the bottom about one foot apart to keep the hog from touching the bottom and also support the bottom of the vat. At the top the 2 x 4 on each side would extend about about a foot from the vat at the four corners, so four people could carry the empty vat. It would be laid perfectly over the trench. The water would be put in the vat according to the water measurements. The vat would secure on both sides with iron rods down in the ground even with the top to keep the vat from moving while scalding the hog. At times we would have hogs weighing four hundred to five hundred pounds or more. Sometime during the process of getting the vat and everything ready and after the water heated up it was time to kill the hog. This is the way we did this, the hogs would be shot one at a time with a 22 cal. short bullet. The shooter would shoot the hog between and in the center of the hog's eyes. When the hog falls out most of the time the hog will be frozen and drop to his knees. The next step, another person will have a long sharp butcher knife and would stick the knife with a sharp pointed blade down the hog's throat as deep as he could. Before he could pull the knife out, the blood would rush out with a great force while the heart was still beating. The more blood that comes out of the hog, the less spoilage of the meat you will have after butchering and salting it down in the smoke house. The hog is shot at the floor pen. Dad would drag the first hog out through the hog pen door. The hog would bleed on the ground away from where it would be cleaned and gutted. The women folks and children would not see this. The hog would be dragged by mule (most farms did not have a tractor) to the heated vat to be put in the hot water. They would kill a couple of hogs at a time.

People used plow chains, laying two inside the vat about 18 inches apart. Each chain would be 20 feet long. On one side of the vat would be a short ramp from the top slanting out away from the vat about three feet all the way to the ground.

This would help slide the hog into the vat. Depending on how big the hog was it took at least four people to get it in the hot water.

Dad would get a small green limb from a pine tree to put in the water while the water was heating up, this would help with the smell. It was easier to remove the hair with two people on each side of the vat. They would take the four ends of the chain from opposite sides and this would help move the hog and each time they would pull back and forth together to tighten on the hog to keep it moving back and forth. This had to be done to keep the hog moving so the hog would not get too hot in one area, this had to be done so the hair would come off the hog easier. Turning or flipping the hog from side to side would take about five to ten minutes before the hog was ready to come out of the hot water. Two ends of the chains would be hooked on one side of the vat, the side the ramp was on as the men pulled the other ends toward the ramp the hog would roll from the vat onto the short ramp to a cotton sheet or boards to keep the hog off the ground. They could tell when the hog was ready to take from the vat because the chains would begin to scrape the hair off the hog. Four people, including the women folks would scrape the hair off as quickly as possible. The head and feet would be the hardest but they would come clean.

The best way to get the hair off was to use Mason jar lids. After removing all the hair, the hog could be hung up. The men would pick up the hog and hang it up to be gutted. Sometimes the hog was too heavy to lift, so they would take a cotton weighter that they weigh cotton with to lift the hog. The cotton weighter would be a two legged pole with the legs spread out about five feet at the ground. The top of the legs would attach and bolt to a strong long pole, this would keep the front of the pole about six feet off the ground while the other end down at the ground. When the ground end is lifted up this would bring the front end to the ground. The hog would be carried to where it needed to be gutted and the cotton weighter would be moved over the hog to be lifted from the ground in order to gut the hog from the tail part between the two hams down the belly area all the way to the hog's throat where it would bleed the rest of the blood from the neck. The hog should be hung up by the heels (back legs) or ham string. This is a strong muscle near the foot. To find this muscle you will cut the back part of the foot area between the leg and foot and pull the muscle out enough to get a short pole similar to a tobacco truck round, trimmed at each end, so it will fit between bone and muscle. By putting one end of the ham string muscle and the other end of the pole through the other leg, it will spread the legs out so the hog can be pulled up and gutted from the tail part. By cutting through the joint, this will spread the hog out, it would be easy to gut from the tail part all the way to the belly, through the shoulder, down to the throat and jaw area. All the way down the belly and between the hams there would be hard cartilage that with a sharp knife and a hammer to tap the back of the knife (this would let the knife cut through the cartilage) and allow the stomach area to open up more as you cut through and down the belly. When you get to the breast bone area another person would have a tub ready to catch the intestines. The other person cut through the breast bone down to the throat while keeping the big tub down at the breast area. The person with the knife would go into the belly cavity area and cut the back tissue that held the heart, lungs, and guts of the hog and everything would fall down into the big tub. This would only leave the two kidneys attached and still in the cavity of the hog, one on each side of the back bone area. These were removed and used in hashlets. Cutting up the hog was a big effort. This person doing this would be someone who had done it before. He had to have some experience or he would rip his hands apart!

We started early on hog killing day about 5:00 in the morning. The temperature was in the thirty's and forty's, that was required. After cleaning and gutting a hog, Mom would always get the tenderloin and brains from the hog to cook for breakfast. She would have her wood cook stove hot for cooking at hog killing time. We had a lot of people to feed. All the neighbors that were helping with the hog killing and their children who were big enough to help

Mom would cook the freshes (lean meat) from the hog and scramble eggs with the brains. She would fix cured ham from last year's hog killing and make a pan full of red eye gravy along with a big bowl of grits, homemade biscuits, and butter with molasses mixed with red eye gravy. Nothing could be any better. She had to cook a lot because she had extra people to feed for hog killing.

The adults would eat first so they could get back to work and then the kids would eat. When they finished she would put everything up where it belongs. Then she would come outside and take her place with the women folks doing what they needed to do.

The Women's Job:

Dad would have a long trench in the edge of the field with tubs, pots, pans, and buckets on the bench and a table that was used for cleaning the chitlins. They would heat two wash pot tubs full of water for cleaning them. This is why we started early. It was a lot of work! First they would take the big chitlin and squeeze the waste material from them and then the small chitlin. They would run hot water in the guts, one lady holding the end of the gut open and the other lady pouring water inside the gut. They had to cut the gut in six to eight feet sections for easy handling. This would give the chitlin the right length for making link sausage. After cleaning the gut good, they would turn the gut wrong side out and scrape them good with a knife or scrapper. After rinsing them off again in hot water they are ready for use, either for cooking or stuffing sausage.

The men folk would take the heart, lungs, and liver and hang it up in the smoke house for one day after hog killing. The women would cook the heart, lungs, and liver in a wash pot or on the flat iron wood stove to make hog hashlet. It would look similar to beef stew with brown to black gravy. This was awesome, really good eating. If the family had a refrigerator, they could freeze the organs (liver heart, lungs) to use whenever they chose to.

The men folk would cut up the hog in sections as needed to make it easy. First they would remove the head. Next they would lay the hog on its back and cut down the length of the backbone. This would let the hog lay flat on its back. They would cut the feet off and give to the ladies to handle them. Some would take the head and cut the ears off. They would take a saw and saw through the upper nose section.

They would take the head and turn the head sideways and with a sharp ax cut the jaw section from the head. There would be a lot of lean meat on the jowls. Then they would take the head and lay it down flat and take the ax and with one good chop go through the head, separating the head in two pieces and that would expose the brain. They would take the brain and put it on ice or in the ice box if you had one. They would cook the brain with eggs every morning for breakfast during hog killing.

Most of the time there would be two men cutting up the hog. The head and jowls can be salted down in the smokehouse with the other meats. Cutting and trimming the hog required skill.

With the whole gutted hog lying on its side, the person would cut all the way behind the shoulder through the backbone area. This would be done the same way with the ham section cut down in front of the hams all the way through the backbone area until his knife cut all the way down to the table. There will be three big sections of the hog lying on the table. Now you have the two hams, two shoulders, and two sides where the ribs are. Where the ribs are attached to the backbone is where the pork chops would be cut from. This is all he could do with his knife at this time. To separate the two hams and two shoulders he used a hand saw to saw between the hams and shoulders. The backbone section that the hams and shoulders were attached to would be salted down in the smokehouse. He then would trim both hams and shoulders to look perfect.

After that he would completely separate both sides with ribs intact leaving the long backbone in one piece. Next with a sharp butcher knife he would cut the top of the back portion. This is where we get our fat back. With skilled hands and sharp knife he would trim the fat back from the back leaving just enough fat on the backbone for the pork chops.

I mentioned the backbone was cut through all the way. The long way on each side is where the pork chops come from. He would take a saw and knife and cut the pork chops the thickness he would like them to be. The tail section at the top of the back between the hams would not be big enough to make pork chops. This piece would be salted down with the head parts. Some of the fat back was cut about one inch thick would be salted down and can be used to make lard. Next he would remove the ribs from both sides. If they had a way to freeze them that was good, if not, they also would be salted down. For years only a few farmers had refrigerators and freezers if they had electric in their homes. If not, the ribs would be salted down and placed in the smoke house.

There would be a lot of meat trimmed from the hams, shoulders, and back area. All the fat and lean meat would be separated from each other and cut up for lard and sausage meat. The skin will be removed from the meat, the fat would be cut up in small pieces, and lean meat would be done the same way. The fat would be put in the wash pot to cook slowly at a light boil to keep from burning the grease. The cooked fat meat would be taken from the pot and would be called cracklins. The skin would be cut up the same way and cooked, this would be called pork skins. The lean meat would be seasoned with sausage seasonings and cut up in small pieces and they would grind it through a sausage grinder to become sausage. Next it would be put in sausage stuffers for making link sausage. The sausage stuffer had a handle for turning and this would allow the top to go down slowly to press against the meat at the bottom. The stuffer has a round opening. The stuffer had this short round funnel that fit and would lock in place at the opening. The small gut would slide up on it all the way. A person would hold the gut end tight with their fingers as someone turned the handle and the top of the stuffer come down pressing the meat with pressure hard to come out the bottom. As the sausage came out and into the gut, this is what they called link sausage. Sometimes the length would be six or eight feet long. When making the link sausage it would be hung up in the smoke house for curing and after a few days drying out this would be dry sausage. This would keep a long time because of the cold weather and by drying it out. This was good eating along with cured ham and other meat that had been salted down. If all this was done right it will not spoil. After cooking the fat, the cooked or dried up pieces were called cracklins. It would be removed from the pot to use for eating on sweet potatoes, putting on biscuits, and corn bread. After the grease had cooled we would dip it out and put it in aluminum cans with a sealed lid on top to use all winter and throughout the year for seasoning and cooking. I can remember the General Store had no cooking oil but they sold lard just like we made in the wash pot.

The skins were cooked in the pot with some pieces of meat. After the skins became brittle we removed them from the pot to cool. The skins did not produce a lot of grease but they were surely good to eat!

The ear, nose, tongue, and feet were cooked and made into souse meat. After hog killing was over, everything would be put back in the appropriate places. The hams, shoulders, side meat, and hog head would be lying on a big table in the smoke house on burlap bags salted down. At the end of five or six days, this is after the meat takes the salt good to the bone to keep from spoiling, then all the meat would be hung up by wire or a strong string. All the salt would be washed from the meat so it would not be too salty. Hanging it would make it harder for the rats and mice to eat through the meat Mom would go to the smoke house and cut portions from the ham and shoulder to cook as she needed it throughout the year.

Growing tobacco:

Sharecroppers started growing tobacco in the early 1800's. They learned how to make cigarettes, snuff, and chewing tobacco from the flue cured tobacco. This became a large source of income for North Carolina and the farmers. The tobacco was here in America when Columbus discovered America. Indians were using it.

First they had to prepare a seed bed for the plants. Dad would find a good spot in a sunny area. He would plow and disk the area up really good so it would be good for sowing the tobacco seeds. This was done around the first of February. It would only take about four ounces of seeds for the plant beds, because they were so small. It took thousands of seeds to make an ounce. Dad's plant bed was thirty feet by a hundred feet. He would put small poles on four sides of the bed to tack down the white linen cloth. He would take the four ounces of seed, mix it with fertilizer, and broadcast the plant beds. He walked up and down the beds with his hands throwing out the seed and fertilizer. The fertilizer would give the seed nutrients to germinate the plant beds! He would use a brush top to sweep the plant bed so the seeds would be down in the dirt. He would take reeds about five or six feet long and stick both ends in the ground. This would leave a hump in the center throughout the plant bed for a little clearance between the canvas and the bed for the plants to grow. On all four sides, the white linen canvas would be pulled tight and tacked to the poles. It would be about 5 months before the plants would be big enough to plant in the ready-made fields.

Farmers would remove the linen canvas from the plant beds in May. This would give the tobacco plants sunlight to grow larger and more robust. While the plants were growing farmers would prepare their fields for transplanting the plants from the bed to the field. The field would have to be plowed under and disked to level and soften up the dirt then dragged down with a drag barrow. The rows would be made with the two-mule cultivator. There was about four feet between each row because they had to be wide enough for the mule and tobacco truck to go down between them. Tobacco slides had no wheels. The tobacco truck has four small wooden wheels. Both have bagging held up by four foot round short poles so that the tobacco will not fall out while the croppers filled them up with the yellow ripe tobacco leaves.

While making the row with a two mule cultivator the fertilizer would be dropped in the row also. The two single disks were about a foot apart that made the furrows for planting the plants.

In the month of May along about the first of the month, farmers transplanted the plants from the beds to the ready-made fields.

The women folk would pull the plants from the beds, and lay them on top of each other side ways. This made it easier for the planting person riding on the planter to be able to pick them up fast each time he heard this little click from the transplanter telling him it is ready for the plant. There would be a person bringing the plants from the beds to the fields. In early years farmers would walk each furrow row to plant the tobacco. This was before the invention of the transplanters. It took three people to transplant the tobacco plants. The two mule transplanter had a 250 gallon tank of water. On top of the water container was a seat for the mule driver to sit. Back behind the big water container was where two people sit one on each side with their legs outward. They would be only a few inches from the ground. The tobacco plants were about eight inches long with a good root system to start growing fast. The plants are laid on a burlap bag in the person's lap. As the mules pulled the transplanter slowly, the two people would drop a plant down into a little trench that the transplanter made as it travels along. The transplanter made a little clicking sound each time you needed to put a plant down. With each click a certain amount of water would come out to wet the roots. At the same time, the trench would be closed as the plant was placed and so on it went. The one bringing the plants from the bed to the field would load each person's lap full of plants.

The tobacco farmers today set out their tobacco in the same way they did back then but the trans-planters are being pulled by a tractor. Today mules are not needed at all for any type of farming. Most farmers did not have a tobacco trans-planter. The trans-planter was owned by the landlord and the sharecropper would use it as their plants got big enough to plant. The tobacco plants would grow fast. After the tobacco plants grew to some height, about a foot, the farmer or sharecropper would cultivate or plow each row and at the same time they would put more fertilizer to the plant. A few days later they would plow or cultivate the field again for the last time and with different plow sweeps, this would be called hilling tobacco. This would be putting more dirt next to the plant for the ground to hold more moisture in order for the plants to grow bigger and grow faster. The plants would grow approximately five to six feet tall and they would have about sixteen to eighteen inch leaves on the stalks. When the plants begin to blossom out at the top and grow "suckers" down the stalk from where leaves grow out from the stalk. At this time farmers would go to the field and begin "topping" and "suckering" the tobacco. This allowed the nutrients to go to the leaves instead of the suckers. The plants would make bigger leaves by "suckering and topping" it (removing the flower from the plant)

Tobacco Worms:

Sharecroppers did not have any type of modern pesticides that they could use to kill the worms. According to past civilization just about any plant had worms, bugs, flies, and so forth. The tobacco plants were no exception they had the worst of the worst. The tobacco worms would multiply fast. This is how the worms came about. There were tobacco flies that would lay eggs on the tobacco plant leaf. They would hatch out in a short amount of days. The eggs would produce hundred of tiny tobacco worms. If they are not destroyed they will eat all the leaves, leaving nothing but the tobacco stalk. They were nothing but an eating machine. The worms would leave their droppings on the ground so it was easy to see. The only way to save the tobacco crop was for all the family members go to the fields and pick the worms from the tobacco leaves. Each person would look on top and under the leaves to find the worms. Most of the time, they were easy to spot because you could see where the leaves had been eaten. We would take and kill them with our feet or we had a bag tied to our shoulder to put them in. When the bag got full we would empty them in a big bucket of lye water or gas. While the tobacco was growing we had other crops we had to plant and cultivate. We barned the tobacco in the month of July and August, this would give us time for other crops. While planting other crops we would still sucker and worm the tobacco crop.

Planting Corn:

The corn rows would be about 36 inches apart. We had a single mule corn planter to plant the corn. The planter had a container on it to hold about a peck bucket of corn. At the bottom of the container it had what you would call cogs to pick up one grain of corn at a time and drop it down the row. Depending how far you wanted to plant the corn apart you would use a different cog. A cog is a metal plate like thing that had little slits around the edge for each grain of corn to fall in, one at a time. Dad would usually plant his corn about one foot apart. The corn would come up fast and about every grain would come up. After the corn got knee high, Dad would have Roy, Laura, and me to hand drop soda hydroxide (a white granular substance fertilizer) by each plant. This would give the plant the nutrients it needed to grow. After about three more weeks we would drop this fertilizer again. While we were doing this, Dad would be going along behind us with the two mule cultivator plowing and hilling the corn. This would be the last time Dad would cultivate the corn. Before he would finish cultivating the corn, Mom would take a big bucket of field peas similar to black eye peas and broadcast up and down a few rows. When Dad came along with the cultivator he would cover the peas in the ground. Mom did a lot of canning of these peas.

Planting Cotton:

After getting the field ready for planting cotton, Dad would use the same planter that he planted corn with except he would change the cog. Cotton would be planted one seed right behind the other to make it come up thick. As the cotton came up and got a little size to it the whole family would go out to the fields to hoe the cotton. This was the same way we did the corn until it got up some size that it did not need hoeing anymore Cotton was easy to grow it did not require much fertilizer and only needed to cultivate it about three times while it was growing. Tobacco, corn, and cotton were mostly what sharecroppers planted for money crops. Later on I will explain the harvest of them.

History of Cotton:

In the Indus River Valley in Pakistan, cotton was being grown, spun and woven into cloth 3,000 years B.C. When Columbus discovered America in 1492, he found cotton growing in the Bahama Islands. By 1500, cotton was known generally throughout the world.

No one knows exactly how old cotton is. Scientists searching in Mexico found bits of cotton cloth that proved to be at least 7,000 years old. They also found that cotton was much like that grown in America today. Cotton seeds are believed to have been planted in Florida in 1556 and in Virginia in

1607. By 1616 colonists were growing cotton along the James River in Virginia.

Cotton is grown throughout the world and has been for thousands of years. Over the period of several years of growing cotton in the New World, people began to understand the importance. Cotton was used for clothing for humans, insulation for keeping things warm, and to keep cold out. Before the invention of the cotton gin by Eli Whitney in 1793, cotton seeds had to be separated from the cotton by hand. This was a slow process. It required more slaves to do this and also pick the cotton from the fields. The cotton gin was a faster means of separating the lint from the seeds. It could separate 50 pounds of cotton while a worker could only separate one pound.

The Cotton gin helped cotton to surpass tobacco in the South as the number one cash crop. The need for more cotton required more slaves in the south. The plantation owner encouraged the slaves to breed and have more babies. This created the expansion of slavery in the South and made the black men slaves high dollar. In the South before the Civil War, by 1850, slaves made up 50% of the population of the Southern state. Today cotton plays a big part in our economy.

The mechanical cotton picker can pick several rows at a time, It would take only about a week to pick 100 acres and in the old days it would take weeks to pick 100 acres with slaves. The cotton picker helped build the South more than people realized.

Growing Livestock Food:

Livestock consist of about any animal that we fed the hay to mules, cows, goats, sheep, even chickens (they loved picking the grain from the hay). The hay field would be plowed and disked and then dragged over with a two mule drag harrow to level the field. During the early years we had no tractors anywhere in our area. We walked behind the plow and drag harrow. I remember riding on the disk. It had a seat on top of it, this would help make the disk go a little deeper in the soil to turn the top soil over this will cut up the weeds and corn stalks, tobacco stalks, or whatever was planted there the year before. We used the same field for growing hay most of the time.

What is Hay:

The hay field would be anything from grass, oats, soy beans, rye grass, (ledpideza), part of these mixtures or all of them, when harvested they will be called hay. About anything that grows in the field that comes up on its own or planted could be called hay because animals will eat most anything.

Dad would mix up the hay mixtures of what he wanted to plant. He would fill a five gallon bucket with seed and walk up and down throughout the field from one side to the other broadcasting the seeds with his hand, refilling the bucket until he finished with the field. After that he would take the two mules and drag harrow and drag the field again to cover the seeds, this is all that was needed for the hay field. Harvesting the hay will come later.

Barning Tobacco:

Cutting wood during the winter for the tobacco barn furnace, neighbors would help neighbors cut wood and haul it to the barn. We would have a big stack of wood cut for barning of tobacco. The pieces would be about four to five feet long so it would go down in the long furnace. The big tobacco flues would run to all four corners of the barn. Families help families barn tobacco, this is what is called swapping labor housing the tobacco. This was your money cash crop. Without a good tobacco harvest it would be hard to make it until another year. So the tobacco crop was the most important crop a farmer had. Usually the tobacco barning season would start in July. We and other families would barn tobacco once a week until it was all out of the field. The women and children would work at the barn and under the shelter or a tree where it would not be so hot. It would take two or three stringers or loopers stringing the tobacco. Depending on how many acres the farmer had.

Each looper that is putting the tobacco on a stick had two to three handers, they would take the tobacco from the handers. The handers would take it from the tobacco truck to hand it. The stem part of the leaf was in their hand. It took about five to six leaves to make a bundle. They would continue handing the bundles to the looper until she got the stick full. While looping the tobacco on the tobacco stick, each end would be resting on the stringing rack. The looper would start at the end of the stick and while she looped the bundle of tobacco it would not take long to get to the other end. There would be about seventy-five bundles on each stick. The stick would be full and heavy. At the end of the rack was where the ball of tobacco string would be. It would be in a can nailed to the end of the rack and as she looped the bundle the string would unwind from the ball. The tobacco leaf is similar to the collard leaf, long and wide with a long stem. By looping the tobacco bundles and holding the tobacco twine tight, leaving one bundle on one side of the stick and looping the other bundle on the other side of the stick, it would equal out two bundles, one on each side. At the end of stick the looper would tie the string around the stick to keep it from coming loose and unwinding.

As each looper finished with the stick, it would be carried over to the hanging racks under the shelter, until the croppers came in at the end of the day. Now everybody would pitch in and carry the tobacco from the racks to be hung up on the barn racks. It would take two men inside the barn, one at the top above the hanger down below. The sticks are handed to a person inside the barn and the person would hand it up to the bottom hanger and every other stick the bottom hanger would hand it up to the top hanger. This way the racks would finish out at the same time.

Croppers in the Field:

Most of the time there would be four croppers in the field pulling leaves from the tobacco stalks. There would be one trucker to truck the tobacco from the field to the barn. It would require two mules, each pulling a tobacco truck with four little wooden wheels or a slide without wheels.

The tobacco slide or truck would have eight four foot tobacco truck rounds cut and trimmed at one end to fit in each of the eight holes four on each side with a nail nailed in the top of each round to hang the burlap bag sewed together to hook on the 4 foot rounds on the inside of the rounds to hold the tobacco in the tobacco truck.

The croppers as the leaves turned yellow week after week would take about three or four leaves off the stalk each harvest day. By doing this, as the leaves got yellow from one week to the other the tobacco leaves would cure out better and leave a yellow shiny silk look. This would bring more money at the market than green leaves (pulled too early) or trashy leaves (pulled too late). When the cropper got one truck filled the trucker would take it to the barn and by the time he got to the barn, they would have a truck empty. He would leave this loaded truck and hook up to the empty one and back to the field he would go. At times the cropper would get ahead of the barn help and have a full truck ahead of them at the barn. If the barn help did not catch up at the end of the day, when the croppers came to the barn, they would pitch in and help them finish. The sled and the tobacco truck were about twenty-four inches wide because they had to go down between each row with mules pulling them. If they were any wider the truck or sled would break the leaves from the tobacco stalks and many times they did. It took a lot of money to raise and barn tobacco and every leaf was precious. With the tobacco row being forty-eight inches apart the trucker had to be careful.

The tobacco barning season would be over in five to six weeks. During the time of tobacco barning each family kept up with their hours. The family that had more hours would be paid from the other family. With more people in some families they would make more hours. The cropper in the field would make about seventy-five cents per hour and this was hot work. The barn help made about forty to fifty cents per hour. Share croppers during the early 1900's had no money except at crop selling time. At this time after selling some tobacco they would square up and pay the families that had more hours.

Curing Tobacco:

The tobacco barning harvest would take about five to six weeks. Most farms only had one tobacco barn. Each week we barned tobacco and at the fifth or sixth day the tobacco had to be finished curing in the barn. Then we took out and carried it to the pack house so the barn would be empty for the next barning day. At the end of each barned day, Dad would fire up the tobacco barn furnace to a low temperature until the tobacco leaves turned yellow. Each day he would put more wood in the furnace and the temperature would gradually go up each day until the temperature in the thermometer reached the about 180 degrees. By the fifth day the fire in the furnace would be put out by closing up the dampers and it could not draw in air and then the fire would go out. Dad would open up both doors on each side of the barn so the cured tobacco would get moisture over night. The sixth day we would take it from the barn and put it in the pack house. As each week went by we removed the cured tobacco from the barn. We would mark each barn so that when we started to grade the tobacco we would take it as it came from the field each week. Sometimes it would take the sixth day before the cured tobacco would be ready to take from the barn. When this happened we would get up about two a.m. on the tobacco barning day and take out the tobacco. We would hang the cured tobacco outside under the tobacco barn shelter so we would have the empty barn to put the fresh tobacco in that day.

The racks under the shelter would be big enough to hold the cured tobacco and what we barned that day. After that day's barning, we would take the cured tobacco from the racks and carry it to the pack house. This was a lot of extra work if we did not get the barned tobacco cured out on the fifth day. Some farms had two tobacco barns because they had more acreage to harvest, but it made it more convenient to have two barns. Each person helped the other with whatever they needed to do because this was their main money crop. There were more children in a family back in the early 1900's. They all played a big part farming while the three months of school was out during the summer. They had to make the best of it. The kids played a big part in harvesting other crops even after they started back to school in the fall.

The barn furnace was a round firebricks and motar mix. About five to six went inside the barn and at the other end it was made where a big round metal tin flue would fit onto it. The flue would go around the inside of the barn and at the end and the back of the barn there was a big smoke stack about six feet long. The flue would go out of the barn at the bottom near the ground and out about two feet from the barn and up. This would draw the heat throughout the barn. The furnace door was made of metal and we could adjust the door damper to how hot we wanted the temperature in the barn. The tobacco barn had a shelter down one side where the furnace was and this was the front. There was also a shelter down both sides of the barn this had to be big because this is where we hung the green tobacco during the barning days. In case of rain the barn help could also get under it until the rain stoped. I can remember in the late forties oil burners came out. They really make it easy for curing tobacco. This was up to the landlord if he put new oil burners in the barn. Some landlords waited as long as they could before they would put in oil burners. If they did not keep up with the other landlords that did put in oil burners the farm would be hard to rent the farm out to sharecroppers! They did not want to saw and chop wood all winter. There were two types of oil burners. One type was four big, big burners in each corner of the barn. The other type was four sets of burners, each having six little burners in each set that were placed in and about each corner of the barn. There was a big two hundred to three hundred gallon drum outside that would hold the kerosene with oil lines running in all directions to the burners inside the barn. We did not use oil burners at this time. Dad would have a little homemade grill and during the time he was curing tobacco he could bar-b-que a chicken. I hated to see the tobacco barning season come to an end because just about every other day we would have bar-b-que chicken. That made it easy for mom because during tobacco barning season she had to come and do the best she could preparing food for us. Everyone only had one hour to eat and then back to the field.

Grading Tobacco:

Grading tobacco was a time consuming job. We had a grading table similar to a long bench for about four different grades. First the tobacco had to be in order, it handled better that way, and laid flat. We would take the tobacco off the sticks and put it on a small table or on a chair next to the grader. Mom and Dad would do the grading most of the time. They would set in front of the bench and between them they would lay the trash leaves. I would take the tobacco off the stick if I was at home because when the grading started I would be in school. The grades of tobacco would be good, average, poor and green leaves. They would look at every leaf. All the tobacco from the farm would be in the pack house by now. Each stick would be piled on top of the other until you had several stacks of ungraded tobacco. As days went on we would build up several piles of tobacco. Each grade was kept separate. All of us would get together to tie the tobacco in bundles. By using the stems you would take an average hand full and take a good soft leave and fold it the long way. Then you would start at the top of the stems and go round and round with it and the rest of the leaf you would slip between the leaves and out the other side. This would make one bundle of tobacco. It would take about ten leaves for one bundle. After a lot of bundles, we would use the tobacco sticks to hang the bundles on ready to load and to be sold.

Ready for Selling:

Before loading up the tobacco we took the tied tobacco and hung it up on the shelter racks for moisture to get it in order over night. Early the next morning we packed the tobacco in the wagon driven by two mules. The Smithfield tobacco warehouse would be on an average about five to ten miles depending on where we were living that year. It would take about three to five hours to get to the warehouse. At the warehouse they would have people there to help you. According to how much tobacco you had to sell that day they would give you plenty of room. You would drive the wagon inside the warehouse to unload. We would unload the tobacco from the wagon and take the tobacco from the stick and lay it down on a basket type tray. The tray would be wide enough, about four feet square. The bundle would be turned inside and the leaves would be turned outward. That way when the auctioneer came by to put a buy price on your tobacco, he could see the color, the silkiness, and how pretty it was.

They would weigh each pile you had on the floor. All the tobacco was laid in rows on the warehouse floor. We would put the tobacco sticks in the wagon because we could use them over year after year. A few sharecroppers had Model

T Ford pickups but the wagon would hold more than the pickup truck. Some of the warehouses were owned by the tobacco company and some were owned by individuals. There would be warehouse charges for you to sale your tobacco. They would charge by the pound, usually this would not be a lot.

The money we received from the sale would be divided in half. The warehouse knew what to do. They would give you your check and mail the landlord his check or he would pick it up.

The Old General Store:

All during the year we traded at the old general store. Each month the store would issue a coupon booklet. It would be forty dollars a month for us. They knew about what amount of coupons (depending on size of family). The coupon would be just like money. You could only use them at the general store. They had one cent, five cent, ten cents, twenty-five cent and one dollar coupons. At the end of each tobacco season and when we started selling tobacco each time we sold we would pay on our debt at the store until it was paid off. The coupons were the same as money. Not only did the store make interest on the coupons, they made money on what they sold to the sharecroppers. They did real good.

Playing Horseshoes:

If we did not have any electric, we used two big lanterns, hung up at each of the shelters. This was a big event because if you were good enough you could make a pocket full of nickels and dimes. None of us had very much money but we had enough to get the game started. The horseshoe stakes were 40 feet apart. The stakes were 15 inches from the ground, legal distance apart. We would gather at the same place every week about two nights a week and play. At this time I was about thirteen to fifteen years old. We all played horseshoes about three tobacco seasons.

I got good at this. I won a lot more money that I lost. Each night I would have a pocket full of change. Some of the kids would borrow money from me to play after losing what they started with. Most of the time I would win it back anyway but they had fun.

One night Mr. Hinton was playing with us. Sometimes he would play and he was pretty good. He married dad's cousin and a lot of us were related on this particular night. After most of us were eliminated it came down to me and Mr. Hinton. He was about 40 years old. Let me tell you now after everybody was eliminated and lost their money the pot was full of change. That night the best man took the pot. The winner takes all. I knew Mr. Hinton was good but I had proved I was just a little better. I will never forget that night playing with Mr. Hinton. This would only happen once in a lifetime. So it got down to me and him, we flipped to see who would go first. I won the first throw. I was hoping I would throw second that way I had a better chance of winning.

I had to throw my first horseshoe where it would flip in the air two times. This way I had a better chance for a ringer than to let it flip fast.

The first throw was a ringer, boy I got excited! I took a deep breath and carefully threw the second shoe, flipping it two times in the air and it went perfectly on top of the other shoe. By that time everybody was on their feet because they knew both of us were good.

Now it was his turn. Mr. Hinton took a deep breath and threw his first shoe it was a ringer on top of my two. I could not believe it! Now this was a match. You could have heard a pin drop in the dirt. Mr. Hinton took a deep breath and threw the other shoe and it was a ringer landing on the three shoes. Four shoes were around that stake perfect to each other. You could not have played them any better than it you placed them with your hands. Mr. Hinton turned to me and just smiled and shook my hand.

He won the pot of money about twelve dollars in change. It was the biggest pot ever back then playing horseshoes. I still won some money that night, but that pot was enough to go with what I had saved to buy me a new bicycle. We all played on until the end of the season along with Mr. Hinton who played sometimes with us. We never had an ending like this one again. Everybody talked about that night as long as I played horseshoes in that neighborhood. All of them said they would not have believed it if they had not seen it. After that I have always said to myself don't think you are the best at anything.

The Mules Tail on Fire:

Along about the same time in this neighborhood of the same year we were barning tobacco with mostly everyone that played horseshoes. There was this kid about seventeen years old who was a funny and mischievous boy. He told me he could light a cigarette lighter behind the mule's tail and when it started farting or breaking wind the gas coming from the mule's tail would light up into a light blue flame. It would keep burning until the mule had expelled all the gas at that time. I told him I have never heard such a thing that it will not burn. He said that he would bet me a dollar that it would. Well it didn't take long for the old mule to start expelling gas. A mule would do it many times in a day.

I primed or cropped tobacco left handed. I am right handed but that was the way I started cropping tobacco. He had the outside row and he said for me to take his row and he would take mine so he would be closer to the mule. By then I had already bet him the dollar and by that time I began to realize that if he is going through all this, that maybe that the mule fart would burn. It wasn't long before the mule started. Real quick he lifted the mule's tail a little and lit the lighter and so help me the gas caught on fire and I lost my dollar. He said well I got a dollar back that I lost playing horseshoes to me. It was worth a dollar just to know this. This wasn't too bad because my shoe shining box was making me a little money on Saturday night. I was a go-getter when I was growing up in my teenage years. A dollar bill was big money

back then. If a kid went to town with a dollar he could buy
a lot of things.

Road Conditions in the Early 1900's:

In the state of North Carolina through Johnston County
we only had two paved single roads. Hwy 301 running
from New York to Miami, FL. The other one was Hwy 70
running from Raleigh and North of Raleigh to the coast
of Morehead City. We have eleven towns running through
Johnston County, but all of them did not have paved roads
running to and through them.

The towns in Johnston County are Archer Lodge, Benson,
Clayton, Four Oaks, Kenly, Micro, Pine Level, Princetown,
Selma, Wilsons Mills and Smithfield (county seat).

Some towns had paved streets and some dirt roads. Most
of them had hitching rails for mules and horses. One side
of the street would be for Model T Fords and the other for
horses and mules.

During the early years most all of the stores were Mom and
Pop stores. As years went by larger stores, company owned,
came about in our area of Johnston County. The larger
cities like Raleigh and Goldsboro had Sears and Roebuck
& Co., the Great Atlantic and Pacific Tea Co. (A & P) Super
Market, Montgomery Ward, and J.C. Penney Co. All these
big stores came about before the 1900's. As years went on
and people began to have more cars, the shopping centers
were being built just outside of town out of the main business district. Roads became better to travel on, people were

making more money per hour. Progress made everything better. Most sharecroppers still did not have inside plumbing, electric, bathrooms, AC units, up to date furniture, washing machines, dryers, refrigerators, and TVs. Houses were being built, subdivisions began to come about. I can remember when I bought my first home, it was in 1962. I paid ten thousand and five hundred dollars for it. It was a twelve hundred square foot home with a car port. It had a furnace with oil heat but no central air conditioning. We used window units. My monthly payment was $62.00.

History of the Mule:

The mule has been around and has existed thousands of years. This hard working animal has played a big part in the human race. Man discovered the mule in the wild and how it came about and how it would be beneficial to man. Even back before horses were used by man, mules existed at that time. It was believed that the wild jackass and a wild female mare produced the first mule. In the wild, different species of one animal would breed with another animal that is not their kind. It was hundreds and hundreds of years before man became aware of what the mule could do for them.

In ancient Biblical times, humans found out about the mule and where it came from. This is the oldest known off-spring hybrid in the animal kingdom known to man. The Jackass male donkey wasn't too small to breed a mare horse in the wilds!

They believed back in ancient times with man's help, they could take a large donkey jackass and breed it to a mare horse and produce a much larger mule. The cross between a male stallion and a female donkey is called a Hinny. That is much smaller than a cross between a female horse and a male donkey. The Hinny wasn't much larger than the mother donkey and it had big ears like the mother donkey.

Depending on the size of the female horse (mare) and the size of the jackass male donkey will determine how big the mule will be. The best looking male donkey was bred to the best looking mare to produce good size mules. On an average a mule weighed about six to seven hundred pounds. With a larger mare horse the mule could weigh up to a thousand pounds. An average jackass would weigh in at about three to four hundred pounds.

Man soon learned that it was best to breed a big jackass to a big mare than to breed a Stallion to a female donkey to produce the best Hybrid (a mule). If it wasn't for the mule, humans would have struggled for thousands of years trying to build and move things. The mule is the most important thing that ever happened to the human race. The mule is the favorite over all the horses for sharecroppers because they are smart enough to train and they are not dumb as they look. Just dumb enough to be trained for the purpose of anything man wanted them to do and they don't forget what they are supposed to do. They are well suited for farming. Mules have stronger muscles and are tougher than a horse. For its size compared to a horse, it can out work a horse and will not need as much water and food as often as a horse. Mules will only eat about half as much as a horse making it cheaper to have. The mule can be trained better and go in smaller places. They have smaller feet and they don't need shoeing like a horse.

Training a horse is a lot different than a mule. A horse at times seems to have a mind of its own. Both animals can be trained to do about anything. They are easy to farm with. They can go between tobacco rows, corn rows, cotton, soy beans, and other planted crops without stepping on the plants better than a horse. They are trained not to step on things and they will watch out for this. With their small feet about half the size of a horse they are perfect for this type of work. They are gentle to kids, adults, and kids can ride a mule.

Are all Mules Sterile (just about 100%)

The female mules have been known to give birth to a foal. This has only happened in a few times that have been recorded. The male mule is completely sterile and has never been known to sire a mule. So two mules can never reproduce! Most female mules are also sterile, but not always. They have actually been successful mating female mules and male horses or a male donkey. The idea is the chromosomes in the male from one of her parents will pair up properly with those of her mate. But it is a rare event for this to happen, only sixty known cases in the last five hundred years. It is extremely rare! The off spring will themselves also be mules.

The U.S. Mule:

Christopher Columbus brought the donkeys and horses to the New World. Mexico was the first to breed horses and donkeys to produce mules in the New World. Mexico used them for a lot of things in their country. The mules did not catch on good until George Washington became the Father of our country and at that time became the first mule breeder. He found out that mules could do more work, live longer, and eat less than a horse. They could travel more miles than a horse. George Washington obtained him five donkeys from the King of Spain to be shipped to Mount Vernon in the year of 1784. The following year the spring of 1785, at Mount Vernon, George Washington had one hundred and thirty working horses and no mules. He had a large plantation with thousands of acres of land and dozens of slaves – a big number of slaves! By 1799, the year President Washington died at Mount Vernon he had twenty-five horses and fifth-eight mules. By 1807 there was an estimate of 850,000 mules in the U.S. Mules became more abundant as years went on and people needed them badly for just about everything.

In the 1840's in Kentucky, a huge quality type jackasses in good health and muscular shaped for breeding purposes could bring up to $5,000.00 dollars on the market. But look how many good mules he could produce from good female horses. During the 1800's with the cotton booming, the number of mules in America was about twenty-two million by 1897. In the year 1923, the U.S. Department of Agriculture issued a publication and gave specific instructions on how to successfully breed good mule stock. On the Old Historic Spanish Trail that connected Santa Fe and Los Angeles trains of pack mules carried two hundred pounds of supplies each between the two cities from 1829 to 1849 faster than horses could. The 2,700 mile long trail was considered one of the most difficult routes to navigate. The mule proved to be the most adapted to travel this distance in the shortest time.

Wagon Trains:

The wagon train would begin in St. Louis Missouri or Elm Grove Missouri most of the time. There would be over one hundred wagons. As they traveled some went by the way of the Oregon Trail until they reached the Nevada California Trail. Wagons crossing the Mississippi took a little time if there were a lot of covered wagons going west. The Mississippi River had a wooden ferry for wagons to cross. After crossing people would all gather together and trail to Missouri and hook up with more wagons. The covered wagons were the main source of travel to carry goods to several towns, states, or territories throughout the west in the 1800's after crossing the Mississippi. This went on for a long time until the Transcontinental Railroad was completed after the Civil War. The railroad made it possible for immigrants to be rewarded land grants, so they recruited people from the U.S. and as far away as Europe to head west by train. The railroad grant purchased land for them if they stayed and homesteaded the land. The wagon train first began heading west in the early 1820's. During the 1850's the gold rush, along with land grants helped build California and the west. All the land in the west was up for grabs, that was just about the way it was in the 1800's and early 1900's. The wagon train lasted until about 1896. The early years were hard to survive. The wagon train had three different animals pulling the wagons, the horse, mule, and oxen. Most of the settlers liked the mule better. The four to six mule team could travel twenty-five to thirty miles a day where as a horse could travel about half the distance. The oxen could travel a little less than the horse because it was slower but well adapted to pull the wagons. The horse had to stop and graze more, this took time and they required more water than the mule and needed to rest more. The oxen was basically similar to the horse, it needed more food and water but could travel on and did not tire as easily. The mule was a tough animal pulling covered wagons. They would use the larger mules for this job. Some weighing nine hundred plus pounds, just a little bigger than the average mule. The mule would eat less, need less water, and would not tire out.

In the west, the stage coach company would prefer larger mules over horses because mules cold travel five to six miles per hour. The horse would give out long before the mule would. The stage coach team of mules would be about six mules pulling the coach. The stage coach relay station would be between fifteen to twenty miles apart, but over tough terrain the relay station would be closer together. This would not tire the horses as much being only about ten to twelve miles apart. Sometimes they would hookup to a new team of mules or horses and sometime the same team would rest and go on to the next relay stations.

Mules in War Time:

Throughout the history of mules and humans, mules played a great part in pre-historic time alongside humans. During the Roman times and King David rein, the mules were used for travel because they could go so long without rest, food, or water. Again they were used in ancient times for riding and to carry war supplies in the year 1040 BC. Mules were famous in Egypt before 3000 BC for work animals and freight hauling in rough mountain area. They were used a lot in deserts because of the ability to travel long distances, for their strength, and could go without water for a long time. Mules played a great part in all the wars, World War I and II, the Korean War, Desert Storm, Afghanistan, and the Civil War. The North and South used millions of mules. Sometimes they got penned down and with a lack of food supplies they had to eat a lot of their mules. So, history tells us that the mules have been a big part of the human race.

Sweet Potatoes:

Soon after we transplanted the tobacco from the plant beds into the field, Dad took the same tobacco transplanter and we planted sweet potatoes. After selling our tobacco crop in the fall, now it was time to plow up and harvest sweet potatoes.

Dad would take a mule and walk behind the turning plow and drive the mule beside the sweet potato row. He had to guide the mule just right to be able to turn the dirt over and expose the sweet potatoes. They would be on top of the ground, on top of plowed up dirt. From then on we would pick the sweet potatoes from the vine roots and lay them in a pile. Then another person with another mule would pick them up and pile them up and down the row and put them in bushel baskets.

Depending on how many you wanted, some sharecroppers planted a lot, two or three acres for selling to people in town and most of the local Mom and Pop stores. We only planted what we could eat. Dad fed the hogs with a lot of them. Actually the sweet potato was not a cash crop in the early years but a few farmers sold some. The average share-cropper did not have enough time to house tobacco, corn, and cotton because these three crops were the money crops, mostly tobacco and cotton.

By the time we harvested the other crops, the cotton picking went on almost until frost before sharecroppers could get it out of fields. The cotton process was slow. After we harvested the sweet potatoes, we would carry them to the house, clean the dirt off them, and put them in a tobacco barn.

It would take about one month for them to dry out just a little. They became sweeter this way. We kept them in the barn away from birds and chickens pecking holes in them. Mom would bake some in the old wood cook stove with homemade butter mixed with molasses and hog cracklins. I don't see how it could get any better. Mom would always have a lot of sweet potatoes and buttermilk biscuits on hand to give to the hobo's, when they came to the house from the railroad tracks.

When the weather began to turn cold, we had a little potato hill near the house to put the sweet potatoes and also the Irish potatoes in away from the cold weather. This is how the potato hill worked. Dad would dig a small area in the ground but not too deep and build a box around it up from the ground about two feet and have it covered with dirt on top and all around it with a little door at one end to open up to remove the potatoes when we needed them. The potato hill would keep them from freezing all winter long.

Oil Burner:

After a few years went by the landlords would have oil burners in the barn. This was a lot better and convenient than to heat tobacco barns with wood! This would work a lot better than the potato hill to keep them from freezing. We only needed to light one burner with low heat just enough to keep the potatoes from freezing. This would not use up a lot of oil.

During the winter if a sharecropper gave out of anything your neighbor would help you to have food. People helped people in those days because everybody had experienced this at some time.

We gave away lots of potatoes, meats, and canned goods to help our neighbor. Nobody had any money. If families did not raise their vegetables and canned them along with some hog meat and put things up for winter it would be bad. Sharecroppers could not borrow any money at the bank because all the banks went belly up during the 1929 depression. The banks were cousious. The bad part about the Sharecroppers was that they did not have any collateral they could borrow money on. Again the only way a share-cropper had any money between selling crops was to pick up odd jobs for the landlord doing things to help him. If the town was near by the wife might find her a little job during the non-farming work helping somebody in their house or with the Mom and Pop stores.

The War Years:

After Japan attacked Pearl Harbor, this turned the whole world upside down and the way a person would think or do things. Manufacturing stopped making cars and all types of vehicles for the public. They turned their production company completely around and started making vehicles, planes, boats, Jeeps, clothes, and everything for the military.

President Roosevelt started getting thing done in a hurry! We were not ready for war. Roosevelt was doing everything fast to save the country. He tried to stay out of the war as long as he could, but when Japan attacked Pearl Harbor ,he knew that we were at war! It wasn't long before the government started to ration a lot of things. Throughout the country the government began to mobilize things quickly. They drafted young men and women to serve in hospitals, supply depots, and lots of other areas where women would be suited to help during the war. Sharecroppers would receive rations stamps during the war. Every American was issued a series of rations books during the war. The rations book contained stamps good for certain rationed items,. Among them were sugar, eggs, bacon, meat, cooking oil, can foods, salt, gas, cheese, rubber, metal containers, coffee, bicycles, silk, and nylon.

You could only buy what your rations stamps called for and how much. Some people got put in jail because they would buy rations books on the black market from crooks and if you got caught buying a book or selling one you would go to jail. Some groups of people someway got their hands on thousands of rations books and sold them throughout. Some got caught and some did not. A lot people believed that a lot of the crooks were working for the government during this time of rations. It was told by a reliable source that some people working for the government got completely rich from the program. I will never forget those war years. I can still remember some of the prices of things.

During this particular time Dad had a Model T Ford. We did not ride very much because we had no money. The gas was nine cents per gallon. The gas pump had no electric, neither did the service stations. The gas pump had a large round glass on top of the tank where down below there was a handle that you moved back and forth when you pumped the gas. The gas would go to the top where you could see the gas.

The big gas container had numbers on it from one to ten. Number one was at the top of the glass. To put gas in your car you would put the nozzle in the neck of your gas tank, turn a little handle and the gas would slowly feed by gravity to go down into your car. Ever how many gallons you wanted, you looked at the numbers as the gas flowed down and stopped it where you wanted to. Most cars would not hold over ten gallons of gas. A person was lucky if he could fill up his tank because you could only get as many gallons according to your rations stamp book or a person did not have the money to buy the gas. At this time we would not have any money to buy gas. Then we would ride the mule and wagon. Most of the time families stayed at home because without any money and a way to go what else could you do?

The Catch Me Eye Explosion:

On March 7, 1942 at 2:57 a.m. an army truck pulling a large trailer with 30,000 pounds of ammunition exploded on Highway 301 just south of Selma, two miles from Smithfield. The explosion killed six people and injured over one hundred. The blast could be seen and heard fifty miles away. People thought that Japan had attacked the U.S. again.

Some thought it was a bomb blast. It was caused when a car collided with the big army truck. They both caught fire. It took about two hours after the accident before the great explosion happened. The truck and big trailer were loaded with gum powder, grenades, and other explosive material to be delivered to the army.

The explosion caused a crater in the concrete highway. It destroyed and damaged buildings, broke windows, more than three miles away a filling station was demolished. This was the only station for miles around. The windows in Selma's homes and stores were shattered and the Selma Cotton Mill lost 900 windows. Most of the Talton Hotel was leveled to the ground. After the fire cleared and officers could see through the debris they found bones from other bodies. Officers found Edward E. Howell of Goldsboro, a taxi driver, and the other body was Jessie Holloway of Goldsboro, NC. Miss Holloway was burned in the hotel room, she survived. Later on they found others killed in the explosion.

I can remember the explosion. I was six years old. Dad and Mom thought we had been attacked by Japan again. We all were scared of what might happen with Japan. The next day the news was on the radio of what had happened and when and where it happened. People from all over everywhere came by mule and wagon and Model T Ford to see the scene and the wreckage of the truck and car or what was left of it. The explosion scattered pieces one mile away. The explosion made a big place in the highway deep and wide.

In a few days the state had convicts filling the big hole with dozens of dump trucks of dirt. The 301 Highway was a busy road at that time because not only was it the main road in Johnston County, this also was the main road that went North and South from Main to Florida. For a long time this area was a place of destruction that most people did not want to see. The blast area stayed that way until some business men in the area started building it back. It took a long time to remove the debris. This was the most traveled road at that time. Today it is one of the busiest intersections anywhere in the state of N.C. This intersection is right off interstate 95 and Highway 70, crosses over the 301 Highway that goes up in the Raleigh area. It took many months to rebuild Selma and Smithfield and also the cotton mill and homes.

War Years:

The war went on and 80 million people throughout the world got killed. The sharecroppers got poorer, I mean poor! Mom had to patch our overalls and Dad put leather bottoms on our shoes. The few rations stamps that we got, wasn't many. It did not matter much anyway we had no money to buy anything with. The only entertainment we had was the table top radio. This was good as long as the battery held out. When they went out you had to buy another set. Neighbors would go to each others' homes to listen to the news about the war and such as it was. The radio had good music and programs. We would listen to Roy Roger, The Lone Ranger, Amos and Andy, Tom Mix, The Three Stooges, Tarzan,

Pistol Packing Mama, Bing Crosby, Glen Miller, and Pinup Girl Betty Gable. Kate Smith, sang "God Bless America". She was born May 1, 1907 and died June 17, 1986 at 79 years of age. She was the first lady of radio. Other songs she sang were "When the Moon Comes Over the Mountain", "The National Anthem", "Climbing Mountains", "We Will Meet Again", "The Grand Ole Opry", she was the greatest ever!

My Dad's youngest brother Albert went to war in 1942. He was drafted into the war at the age of 22. He went to Camp Shelby located along Highway 49, just outside Hattisburg, Mississippi. After his training the Army sent him to the Philippines. He fought through several battles and never got wounded. The American and Philippine forces fought together defending their Island from Japan. There were no victories during the war. The Japanese surrounded the island and many Americans became prisoners, what didn't die. After dropping the atomic bomb on Hisoshima and later on Nagasakt, Japan announced on August 15th that they would surrender. They signed on September 2, 1945, the unconditional surrender of all the Japanese armed forces. The fighting in the Philippines came to an end. I can remember how happy everybody was when Uncle Albert came home. It was hard times after the war with all the armed forces coming home together with families and wife's. Uncle Sam passed the G.I. Bill that was promised a great many benefits for the Veterans. They established hospitals, low interest mortgages for homes, and paid for them to go to college. Eight million World War II Veterans went to school between 1945 and

1956. It backed home loans, gave Veterans a year of unemployment benefits, and they had medical care.

This all helped the economy to grow and put more people in the working force. President Roosevelt signed the G.I Bill into law in the year of June 1944. Not everyone agreed with this because they thought this would be too much money to spend while the war was taking its financial toll on the American people . It cost our government 145 billion dollars over all for the program, but the Veterans took advantage of this and a lot of the Veterans did not. The Veteran that did take advantage of this G.I Bill made a lot more money than the Veteran that did not. The tax revenue from the participation of these Veterans paid for the cost of the G.I Bill plan over and over again. This ended up a good thing for the late President Roosevelt who submitted this bill to Congress and was passed. Times were hard before the war. It took a long time during the Presidencies of Harding, Coolidge, President Hover, and President Roosevelt. It was after World War II before America got on their feet.

During Truman presidency they showed some signs of the economy recovery and by the late 40's and early 50's the economy began to improve fast! It showed more signs of improvement than in the human history. President Theodore Roosevelt was the only president in American history to serve three terms and started on the fourth. He died in the year April 12, 1945 in Warm Spring, Georgia at the age of 63, with a hemorrhage. Harry S. Truman succeeded him and ended the war with the surrendering of Germany to the Russia and Japan to the U.S.

Back to Planting Cotton and Harvesting Cotton:

It was easy planting cotton. Dad would use a little cotton planter pulled by one mule. The cotton rows were about three feet apart. He would start on one side of the finished field for planting. He would have an attachment sticking out from the planter. One end or part of it would drag the ground three feet from the row he was planting. When he planted the second row he followed the mark it made on the ground from the first row. This would give the cotton rows the right distance apart. Then on and on he went until he finished the planting, except for stopping from time to time to put cotton seeds in the planter. It took a good mule to walk straight the way you pointed him to go.

The cotton was the easiest crop we had to plant. We only cultivated it about twice during the growing season to keep most of the grass from growing. After the cotton stalks got some size, about 2 to 3 feet high, the blossoms would appear and then the cotton ball behind the flower. About one month the balls would open up and they would spread apart about the size of a baseball. This is when the cotton would appear. The cotton would hang there a long time before picking. Some farmers would pick their cotton before harvesting hay. But some would wait until almost cold weather started, depending on the other crops or things the farmer had to do. There was one good thing that cotton would be there when you got ready to house it. Picking cotton was hard work, it would be a long time before the mechanical cotton harvester would be ready for the farmer to use. Picking cotton by hand was the only way it could be done.

Things We Would Do When Picking Cotton:

The first thing would be a cotton sheet. The cotton sheet would be made of burlap bags, they were clothe bags made from just about anything. It could be an onion bag, potato, fertilizer, corn, beans, and hog feed bags. You would split them open and sew about four together and it would be about the size of a bed sheet. You will need a bag to put the cotton in as you picked. These bags would also be made out of burlap bags. This bag needed to be about five feet in length and about three feet around. It had a strap sewed on to it and you would put this around your shoulder. Picking cotton was a back breaking job. The bag would drag at your side and behind you. You would pick the cotton and it would take a while to fill up your bag or it got too heavy to pull, then you would have to empty it. The cotton sheets would be at the end of the rows. You could carry it or drag it to the end of the rows and empty it on the cotton sheet.

At the end of the day you would tie up the sheets. This would now take two people to do this. One would get at a corner of the sheet and across from him the other person would get that corner. Both would reach across the cotton on the sheet and hand the other person their corner. They would pull hard and tie a knot with the one corner and do the same with the other corner.

It had to be a good knot because when you weighed the cotton, the sheet must not come apart. The weigher we had was a tee handle type, where you would lift up the backend of the pole and let the other end in front of the pole down to where the cotton sheet was. The scales would be at this high end off the ground. The tee handle scale will be attached to the pole with a hook made with the scales and it would have a bottom hook to hook to the cotton sheet. The whole thing would be made up with two long legs about four feet apart at the ground and about six feet high. The other end would be attached to the pole by raising the tail end of the pole to lower the front so it can reach down and hook it to the sheet of cotton. This is the same type of scale we used for lifting the hogs at hog killing time.

The average person could pick about 200 pounds of cotton a day. This is almost unreal because cotton is light. What helped the cotton to weigh more is because the cotton you picked has cotton seeds mixed in with the cotton! This is where the cotton gin came into play. The cotton gin separated the cotton from the seeds and if there were leaves or trash mixed in with the cotton, it would remove them from the cotton. After all this done the cotton gin would pack the cotton with its machine into a tight bale of cotton with a burlap cloth material around both sides and the bottom leaving the top exposed.

(Cotton is ginned and baled about the same way today.) They were heavy and weighed in at about four to five hundred pounds. It would take about a thousand pounds or more of cotton to make a bale.

So you see that the cotton weighed about what the seeds weighed. I can remember when I was twelve years old I picked 192 pounds of cotton in one day. As I got older, I could pick way over 200 pounds in a day. Boy this was back breaking. A good cotton picker could make more money but it was harder work than working in tobacco.

Barning tobacco workers only made thirty-five cents to fifty cents per hour, field works hands made seventy-five cents per hour barning tobacco. The farmer would pay $2.00 for 100 pounds of cotton. So two hundred pounds would be four dollars. A farmer would sometimes need help picking cotton because of certain types of hardships or not being able to bend over to pick their cotton, it could create a problem.

During this time picking cotton was after barning tobacco so the sharecroppers would not have a hard time finding help. A sharecropper would have to give half the money out of the cotton when sold to the landlord

Keep in mind the sharecroppers had to give half of the tobacco and cotton money to the landlord. The landlord expected you to have a good crop so it would bring in a lot of money. The only three things you did not have to split with the landlord were your corn, hay, and sweet potatoes.

Back to Planting and Harvesting Corn:

Planting corn would be similar to planting cotton, to be exact the same cotton planter pulled by one mule is what you would use for planting corn. Dad had to adjust the cogs, the gears in the planter, for how fast he wanted the seeds to come out of the planter. Planting cotton with the planter you would move it less than how you would sow the cotton. The seeds will be close together and the cotton would come up thick. With corn Dad would adjust the planter for the seed corn to fall about 8 to 12 inches apart. When it grows and the tassels begin to come on the stalk it needs more room for pollination to make larger ears of corn. Corn needs a lot of rain to make big ears and a lot of nitrate consisting of potassium this type of fertilizer will make corn grow fast and produce big ears. With the proper rain fall from the time you plant the corn until the corn develops will take about six weeks to two months. When the corn begins to fill out some of it can be pulled to cook on the cob or cut off the cob.

You have to know when to pull the corn. You take the end of your finger nail and mash the grain at the end where the tassel is. If it pops, the ear is right for cooking. It takes a few weeks for the corn to be picked from the field. It must be dried out and the corn grain must be hard for shelling before you harvest it from the field. Keep this in mind, back in the thirties, forties and early fifties we did all this by hand. Now farmers have all types of machinery and harvesters to do it all.

When we harvested our corn, we would pull it from the stalk and make small piles in the field about every two rows apart. After that a day or two later we would use the mule and wagon and go down the rows and pick up the piles. When the one horse wagon got full we would take it to the pack house to unload. By this time we are through with the tobacco and the pack house is empty. We usually put the corn on the bottom floor of the pack house. Just about all pack houses had upstairs rooms for keeping hay and to feed livestock down below (this will be explained later). A farmer could do a lot of things with corn. There was a corn mill we took it to. The mill would shuck the corn and grind it up into chicken feed or hog feed. Chicken feed would be small granular pieces for the chickens and biddies. Hog feed would be in a powder form like hog supplements. This is important for small pigs and fattening the hogs for winter kill. Also this would be good for biddies and chickens. Corn can be eaten just about any way you wanted to feed it to the livestock.

We had a turned handle corn sheller that we used for shelling corn. First we had to shuck the corn and then after getting a pile of shucked corn, we would shell a lot of it to feed the chickens during the winter and summer. The mules, cows, and hogs could eat the corn on the cob. Sometimes it would interest me just to watch how the animals ate their food.

Harvesting Hay:

We had a few acres set aside for our hay field. The hay field would consist of soy beans, rye grass, and just grass that grew up along with the other things. We would broadcast the field with the grain and let it grow at will. There was no farming of this. We would fertilize the field and when it matured, we would use a two horse mowing machine to cut the field.

The mowing machine had a long arm that you would let down about two to three inches from the ground and it had thin short cutting blades along with length of the arm. The arm was about five feet long. The mower was chain driven on a wheel for the blade to go back and forth. The faster the mules went, the faster the blade would go back and forth. We had to be careful not to fall from the seat in front of the blade. After cutting all the fields we would let the hay lay in the field for about a week to dry. At this time soybeans were mostly planted for animal food. Later on, about twenty years, companies started using more soybeans for food for humans and making soybean oil for cooking. In the late 50's, things really started happening in our country. This became a big movement at this time. More people started having electricity, running water, bathrooms, electric stoves for cooking and heating in the home, fans, AC, and more electric things.

I can remember the first TV set. I saw it in a department store in Goldsboro, NC. This was the year 1950. It did not take long before people had them in their homes, the ones that could afford them. You could only get a few stations, about three or four. You had to use a tall antenna on top of the house and the TV was not yet all that clear. These were black and white pictures for a long time but eventually they got the pictures better. After the news went off there were only a few stations that stayed on the air until about 8:00 p.m. Mostly the TV at this time was for the news and for short movies. The TV would sign off and become a blank screen until the next morning.

Back to Harvesting Hay:

My brother Roy and I would use a one horse wagon to remove the hay from the fields. We were just small kids, Dad might help a little. This was a dirty job. To me the worst job on the farm. There were mechanical hay bailers, but Dad did not use one. Only the big farmers with a lot of cows mostly used the big hay bailers. Roy and I would load the wagon with pitchforks, this was after I got about ten years old until I finished high school. We would jump on the wagon at times to pack it down so we could carry a bigger load. When we got to the pack house, the hay had to be put upstairs and packed all the way to the back and packed high and deep. This is what we fed the mules with, along with ears of corn. We would have to lift pitch forks full of hay and throw it in the top of the loft. This was hot work. This was in the fall around October and just before cotton picking time. The hot straw would fall down in your eyes and down your back. This would make you itch and scratch really bad. It would take several days to remove all the hay from the field.

But before we harvested the hay from the field, we would borrow a hay rake driven by one mule to rake the hay in long narrow rows. This would make it easier to put it in the wagon.

The rest of the hay in the field that the pack house would not hold, we made hay stacks in the field. Dad would take a long pole, about twelve feet high and put one end in the ground with hole diggers. Roy and I would take the rest of the hay in the field and put it around the pole with the bottom bigger and wider around and as we went up with it, it got smaller. Again this was dirty and hot work. After using up most of the hay in the barn feeding it to the mules, we would from time to time, take the wagon, load it with the hay from the haystack, and carry it to the pack house like we did before "feeding the mules".

Upstairs in the pack house we had a cut out floor section above the mule stable where we fed the mules with hay. Dad had built wood racks with slats apart where the hay would drop down in and the mules could pull it through the slats. Each slat was about two feet apart and about six feet across.

Downstairs the mule had a corn box. We had a window hole section cut out and the corn box attached to the side of the building below the window area where we would shuck the corn and put all the whole ears in the box for two mules. We fed them morning and night. This is what we fed the mule with hay and corn. We kept plenty of water in the lot for them. We had to be careful and let the hay dry out good in the field because if it did not dry out if would mold in the barn. This would make the mules sick and could kill them. The big commercial farms that had lots of acreage for hay would raise hay to sale. To make it easier, they would bail the hay with mechanical hay bailers. By doing this the hay would be in bales each tied with bailing wire to make it easy for handling and hauling. The large farmers would sell their hay to the general store and the livery stable.

Livery Stable:

Livery stables played a big part in the farming business. This is where farmers went to buy their mules. Every few years, you would take your old mule in for a younger one to farm. The mule would be trained to work the fields with the farming equipment. Mules were easy to train, the more you farmed with them, the better they got!

I can remember my first tractor in the area. I was eleven years old and this was in 1946. Then about ten years later, more people had tractors to farm with than mules. This would increase more acreage you can farm and made it easy for farmers with tractors, you could use less people on the farm.

In the 50's more and more people left the farms to find jobs in towns. In the early 60's a few little shopping centers started to come about. Back during the early 50's I can remember the first supermarket. This was the Great Atlantic and Pacific Tea Co. known as the A & P Super Market. The A & P became the largest retail in the world, even bigger than Sears Robuck and Co. and General Motors. Slowly after many years, there were less and fewer of them and today they don't exist anymore. It makes me wonder, how can a company be the largest and then go out of business! In my opinion they did not keep up with the times and management played a big part.

Mostly people that owned their land bought tractors first and only a few sharecroppers bought their tractors. Sometimes the landlord would buy a tractor for sharecroppers to use taking turns using the tractor for certain things.

Corn Fodder:

After all the corn was harvested and before a farmer or sharecropper cut the corn stalks, some of them may decide to rip the corn leaves from the stalks for mules, horses, and cows for extra food. To be on the safe side they would take the leaves several at a time and take another corn leaf to tie the fodder into a bundle. The fodder did not have much food nutrients because they were completely dried out. This was food that would help feed the animals if other food became in short supply.

During the time the corn grew and matured and the corn grew on the stalk and developed into ears of corn which would be green and before it started drying out, sharecroppers would cut the whole stalk down and load it up on the wagon and feed it to the animals. The reason they did this was because the animal food was giving out from last year. A sharecropper would rather do this than go in debt to buy feed for their animals at the end of the year after selling their crops. They would not have another farm bill to pay until the next year. There was several ways a farmer could use the fodder, by making hog beds, cow beds, and putting some in the mules' stables for them to lay on. All share-croppers didn't waste much, he could not afford to. The best he could do was pay out of debt and be debt free when he started farming for the next year. Believe me everybody was poor.

Corn Stover:

Corn Stover consists of the corn stalk, leaves, cobs, and corn fodder which is made from the leaves after the corn in harvested from the stalks. The stalks are left in the fields for a short while to be harvested and used for cattle feed along with other feed that the cows would eat. Corn Stover is a very common agriculture food as well as the non-grain (ear of corn) cob part of the harvest corn. Any animal can eat the Corn Stover. Lots of dairy farms and big farmers use this type of (hay) like material to make their other feed last longer. This is a good hay substitute. Farms would bale up this Stover material in big bales, they would be big bales of hay. All the corn stalks along with some grass in the field would make up the bale. The bales would be left in the field for some time and as the farmers or dairy farmers needed them, they would haul a few to the barn for feed.

What is Corn:

Corn is one of the oldest grain crops that we use in so many ways today. This is historically grain that the Mexicans used 7,000 years ago. Corn is known as America's biggest crop and a source of global food supply. Corn can be made into cornmeal and numbers of other ways for human and animal consumption.

These are only a few of ways corn can be used: grits, corn-flakes, oil, corn bread, deep fry batter, corn flour, pancakes, donuts, baby food, hominy, corn liquor, used in Penicillin, corn starch, corn syrup, starch, and the marvel of corn can go on and on. Corn was in America before Columbus and the Indians used corn.

Corn Cobs:

The corn cob might seem to be the throw away part of the corn. They have their usage and more usages are discovered all the time. Ground up cobs are used for livestock feed. A long time ago corn cobs were used for toilet paper substitute. Corn stalks are starting to be used to produce ethanol gas and you can still make corn cob pipes for smoking!

Run Away Mule:

When I was eight years old, Brother Roy was 11, and our cousin Ed Carter was 10, Dad had us to pick up corn in the field. It had been pulled a couple days before and put in small piles about every other row.

We all three were mean and when we got together just about anything could happen. This was on a Saturday back in the year 1943. Dad had us to hook the mule to the wagon, pick up the corn as we pulled it from the stalks, and put it in little piles to be picked up. We went to the field and loaded up the one horse wagon and did as much as we could do for the day.

Roy hooked the mule up to the wagon and we were off to the corn field. On the farm a child had to work at an early age. Everything was so slow back then. Farming with mules, there was not much danger of getting hurt. This was a good mule, she was slow and all you had to do was tell her to get up (to go) and wow (to stop). You did not even have to be in the wagon, she would do what you told her. She was slow walking and we had no problem with her because she was real gentle around us kids.

It took a while to fill the wagon with corn. After filling the wagon we took it to the pack house to unload. Roy had a seat across the front of the wagon and the rest was open space for hauling.

We worked all day and it was hot. We had made two wagon loads and the mule got slower and slower. We had time to make one more load before dark. Roy would set up front on the wagon seat to drive the mule, Ed and I would sit on top of the corn.

The mule was so slow Roy tried to make her run back to the field with an empty wagon, but she only took a few steps and back to the slow walk. "I can see us now sitting on top of that load of corn."

We finished loading the third load of corn and Roy got in the wagon to drive the mule. Ed and I jumped on top of the corn and we were off with the last load of corn for the day. Roy drove the mule out of the corn field and got in the path that led to the house. We were about a quarter mile or less from the pack house.

Along the way Roy stopped the mule under a big pine tree that was close to the path. It had big green pine thorny pinecones on the ground. Ed asked Roy, why did he stop? We didn't know this but Roy had seen another older mean cousin do this. Ed and I did not know about this and what Roy was going to do. It was a surprise to us. Roy told us that he was going to make the old slow poke mule go faster. Ed said it won't run and you can't make it go any faster. Roy said watch this. Roy jumped down from the wagon and picked up one of those big green thorny pinecones and got back in the wagon. The little wagon seat was right behind the mule's tail, only a short distant.

He took the mule's tail and raised it up a little and stuck the green pinecone under the mule's tail right in the spot. When the mule felt this she put her tail down hard and she squeezed her tail down hard on that hard green pinecone and when she did that it was a lot of force on that pinecone.

The mule jumped like a rabbit. Never would I ever have believed it if I wasn't there because the mule was so slow, it took off so fast Roy had no control of her. It was all he could do to stay in the wagon bouncing and sometimes it was going so fast it was hard for Ed and I to stay in the wagon. About that time the tail gate of the wagon fell out and we both rolled out of the wagon with the corn. We managed to look up at the run-away mule. We could see Roy bouncing up and down in the wagon and hanging onto the seat. He had no control the mule did what she supposed to do because she was scared.

We were about half way to the pack house and watched the wagon. The mule went straight to the stable door and stopped. We never knew what happed to the big green pine-cone, we looked for it but could not find it.

Dad heard the wagon and came out of the house and wanted to know what happened. He could see the corn that fell out of the wagon and could see Ed and me walking up to the pack house from the field. I don't know how Roy thought to tell Dad this quick. Roy told Dad that some bees stung the mule and there were a lot of them. Roy did not want a beating from Dad's belt. Ed and I never said a word, we were too scared to. Dad believed this story right on up until he died and he died in March 1983 at 80.

Figure 1 The Author's paternal grandparents, Charlie
Woodard and Nancy Ellen Woodard (Miss Nan)

Grand Mom Woodard:

Every Christmas we all would go to our Grand Mom
Woodard. My Dad was one of seven children, he was the
oldest. There were a total of eighteen grandchildren. All of
our relatives were close to each other and all my cousins
seemed like my brothers and sisters. My Mom and some of
my Aunts would help Grand Mom prepare the meals, do
the cooking. Grand Mom had a flat wood cook stove and
it had a big wide top. She also had a big living room heater
that would burn coal. She would use this coal heater along
with the wood cook stove to cook her meals. They would
start preparing the meals around 10:00 a.m. and hope to
have it all through by 12:00. All of the cousins would play in
the yard until dinner was ready to eat. The adults would eat
first and according to our age, that is how the grandchildren
would eat. After everyone got through eating, we would all
go outside to play. We would all play softball. This would
take most of us playing ball.

Late in the afternoon we all would come in the house and get
ready to head home. Home was not a long way off for most
of us. Before we all left to go home, we all would exchange
Christmas gifts. My Uncle Tommy was the Santa Clause.
Every Christmas my Uncle James would bring a big stalk
of bananas and they were big. It had close to 200 bananas
on it. He would hang it up on the front porch and anytime
you wanted a banana you just pulled one off.

At the end of the day most of them were eaten. Everyone
was pleased with their gift. All families were close to each

other. We all looked forward to Christmas because this was about the only time during the year that we would get any fruit and a gift. After selling the crops in the fall this would be the last money that you could get your hands on.

Cotton would be the last thing that sharecroppers had to sell late in the fall. We picked our cotton early but not too late in the fall and had it ginned into bales of cotton and kept the bales late in the fall before we sold them. This way the cotton prices will go up per pound and this would be worth waiting this late to sell your bales of cotton. A bale of cotton would weigh about 400 pounds. It wasn't long after the first of the year that everybody was broke again.

To get a part time job was almost impossible because there were no factories and businesses around in the neighborhood. If you even had a way to go to town to find a job, most likely you would not find one.

If you were lucky, a person might find a job with the landlord doing repair work on the different farms he had. There was repair work that needed to be done on tobacco barns, pack houses, helping neighbors cut wood for the home, and tobacco barns.

There would always be a job cleaning out the mules' stables. I can remember mostly when I was a young kid, from about eight years old until I finished high school this was my job in the winter months. Boy this was a bad job. I had to use pitch forks to get the hard press manure with straw mixed with it and load it on a tobacco truck and carry it to the field to be scattered.

Some neighbors needed you to help saw their wood for next year. There were no chain saws. We used a cross cut saw about six feet long with a handle at each end. One would push while the other one at the other end of the saw would pull this was how it was done (push and pull).

We sawed oak trees down they would make the best fire wood. Then it had to be sawed up in the right length for the tobacco barn, cook stove, heater in the living room, and for killing hogs.

In the early years there were about four cars in all the families. The rest of us went by mule and wagon. It would be close to dark before we would get home. We always carried a lantern with us and if we met a car or another wagon we could tell how far away they were from us.

From time to time we would go to Grandmom's house. Grandmom had a big gray rooster. If he was out of his chicken coop, he would run us down and try to jump on us. He would use his spurs to hurt us and sometimes he would succeed and bring blood from you, if he hit you with his spurs. We had to stay clear of the big gray rooster, by being careful, this would only happen a few more times.

A few weeks later, on Sunday, we all went back to Grandmom's for dinner. We all took turns at the table and when all the kids finished our meals Grandmom asked us how was our chicken and pastry? We all agreed that it was good. She said that we would not be bothered by the big gray rooster again. Some of us said why did you sell the rooster Grandmom? She said no, that we all ate him for dinner!! We never thought that would happen. Just imagine eating that rooster!

The Fish Man:

Every Friday or Saturday the fish man would come by with his boxes of fish. He travelled with a little Model T Ford truck. I can remember this at four or five years of age before I started school. He had lots of fish, trout, flounder, spots, and others. We would all look forward to him bringing fish each week. He would have drinks, candy, and corn meal. In order to have money when the fish man came, Mom would sell butter, eggs, and whatever she could to get the money to buy the fish. Mom managed to have money every time he came. There were six of us in the family, L.B., Roy, Laura, myself, Mom and Dad. The fish man charged 15 cents and 20 cents per pound depending on what we bought. Drinks were 5 cents and candy bars were 3 cents. If Mom had any money left we would buy candy and drinks. She would buy about 5 pounds of fish. The best that I can remember, Mom paid about $2.00 for everything. This was before and after World War II. Most people did not have a car, travel was done by mule and wagon, a one mule hover cart, walking, and a bicycle. We were already poor, but during the war years we all got poorer. We did a lot of fishing at the river, but the fresh water fish were not as good as the ocean fish.

During the War:

While the war went on most everyone had Ration Books. We could not buy a lot with the few Rations Stamps we were issued. Most families did not have the money to use up all their Ration Stamps. Some people could not travel by car because they had no money to buy gas. A lot of the share-croppers would remove their rear axle and wheels from the Model T Ford and make a hover cart with it. This would ride better than the wagon because of the rubber tires.

The seat would be big enough for two adults and maybe a small child. This went on for a long time. After the war, they would put the axle back under the Model T Ford. By this time we could buy gas if we had any money because the Ration Stamps were not used anymore.

The car factories began to make cars again. There were only a few made in late 1945 but by 1946 all factories were back in business.

Going to Church:

Mom took us to church when the weather permitted. We had to walk a short distant, less than a mile. Mom taught us to say our prayer when we went to bed. The prayer was – "When I lay myself down to sleep, I pray the Lord my soul to keep, if I should die before I awoke I praised the Lord myself to take. Amen".

A few years later, I can remember going to this church in the country, a few miles from Micro. This was a little white church and was in the 40's. It had electric lights and a fan in the window. The fan did not do much good in the summer. When we got to church, the windows would be up and all the doors open. I believe it got as hot as 100 degrees sometimes. The name of the little church was Parrish Memorial Baptist Church. In each pew they had six to eight little face fans that helped a little but it was hot. When we left the church and went home it was not much better. In the winter we had a coal heater at church. Mr. Charles Watson was a Deacon and he would have the church warm on Sunday morning. It was nice going to church in the winter.

Once a year we had Homecoming. We had tables made out of boards and wire tied to a tree on the outside. They would use table cloths to cover the boards the best they could. Everyone would bring food and that would be the biggest meal of the year. Everyone from miles away would always turnout for Homecoming. You would not get a meal like this until the next year!

Baptism:

The church had a special place down at the river where the water was shallow and it had a sandy bottom. Everybody went to see the baptism.

Keeping the Yard Clean:

Back in the early years, people had no type of lawn mowers. Most people kept their yard clean from weeds and grass by hoeing the weeds with the hoe. We had these big yard brooms. They were made from dogwood branches. Each Saturday Mom and Dad would sweep and clean the yard.

Mom would go with us to gather dogwood branches because they had to be the right size and the right length. She would trim them up and put enough of the together to do a good job.

In the late 40's and early 50's, people changed their way of thinking about their yards. People began letting their grass grow out after the push mower came out and a few years the gas mower. I can remember the first push and gas mower that I saw in town. People began to let the grass grow in their yards because it was prettier to see the smooth cut grass than a naked yard. In the 50's things began to change.

The Car:

People started building new homes. Sharecroppers had better farming equipment to farm with there were more tractors in the fields. People were making more money and they had better clothes. The car factories began building better cars with turn signals, stop and tail lights, and with a key or pushbutton start to crank the car engine.

During this time in the early fifties, most cars and trucks did not have air conditioners and heaters. Before turn signals the way you would let other cars know what you were going to do was if you were going to make a left turn, right turn, slow down or stop, you would have to give turn signals with your arm. The up position was a right turn, straight out was a left turn, and down beside the door was to slow down or stop. Most of the roads were narrow, dirt, bumpy roads and cars were not made to go fast.

I can remember my first car, a 1949 Ford Flat Head V-8 engine that I worked and bought it while in high school.

It was not required to have insurance in the early years on up until the fifties. My Dad drove all his life without any drivers' license or insurance. Dad can remember when cars came out in Johnston County, NC. He told us when the early Model T Ford came out they would be packed in crates from the factory. The Dealer would assemble them together and then you could buy one.

The first car in the US was made by Henry Ford and by the 1920's General Motors and Chrysler began making cars. This was the three companies that manufactured in the US for a long time. It was the year 1908 when Dad saw the first car come out in Johnston County, NC. It was priced at three hundred dollars and $20.00 to put it together.

The only roads back then was mostly dirt roads and some old stage coach roads. The horse and buggy could almost run faster than the Model T. Ford. It would take many years before cars found its place in Society. The stop signs and speed limit signs did not come about until the late 20's and 30's. By 1918 all states required you to have car license plates.

By 1935, the year I was born, only 39 states required driving licenses. Most of the time a person did not have to take a driving test. In the state of NC applicants were required to be sixteen years old, pay $1.00 for the driver's license, and did not have to take a written or driving test. All there was to it was for your father or mother to approve to obtain a driver's license. It was not until January 1, 1948 that an Examination for a driver's license was required.

Before the Examination there was no age limit on who could drive. A person could drive as long as you had a good driving ability. Before 1935 thousands of deaths had occurred on state roads and the vehicle had become a killing machine. The cars came about faster than the state could build good roads. Most all roads were dirt roads. There were some brick and board roads in some areas of North Carolina.

Most cars only travel 30 to 40 miles per hour. Lots of times the roads were so narrow that you had to slow down and almost stop if you met another car or a mule and wagon.

Lots of people died because it wasn't the car going too fast, it was because there were no stop signs or stop lights back then. There was no electric to put up stop lights. People could not see any danger until danger saw them first.

People could not see at night because some cars had no head lights, only oil lanterns. When you did see the other car or the mules and wagons it was too late. Things had to get better fast. The car or killing machines were here to stay. It took many years before the roads could catch up with the cars.

My Money:

I have never been afraid of work. The only way I had any money to spend was to work for it. At seven, I worked around the tobacco barns during tobacco season by keeping the tobacco sticks piled up near the stringer or looper so that she could get one quick. I picked up trash and would help hang the full sticks of tobacco in the outside tobacco racks.

I was not counted a full hand, where you would get paid 35 cents per hour. I became noticed of what I was doing out of their kindness, sometimes a person would give me a nickel or dime, I well earned that. This would give me enough to buy a Pepsi and a candy bar for a dime. I could buy a big 4 ounce Baby Ruth. They would cost about $2.00 now, but it would not be 4 ounces.

If and when I went to the movie I could see the movie for a dime, buy a Pepsi and a box of pop corn for a dime "nickel each". When I came out of the movie I would give back the empty Pepsi bottle and get one cent back. This was not a bad deal for only 19 cents going to the movie.

A few years later the movies went up to 14 cents for the movie but the Pepsi and pop corn stayed the same price. Most of the time, I would go early enough so I could see all the movies twice.

People told me that I was a smart little boy. At ten years of age, I did not have to be told what to do. I had good common sense of figuring out things.

I was better off financially when I was getting paid a nickel or a dime that people handed to me than being a regular hand at ten and making 35 cents per hour. I fitted in with my family and we swapped barning tobacco. After the barning tobacco ended, in about six weeks, the families would figure up the hours and if we did not make more hours helping them they would not owe us any money, we would owe them.

To help make ends meet Mom would sell a chicken or some eggs from time to time. During this time in the early years Mom and Pop Stores would buy just about anything you had to sell them. Those stores are gone now.

I helped Mom with the chickens, by cleaning out the chicken coup and putting the manure in the garden. From time to time Mom would give me a quarter.

Outhouse! Move to Kenly, NC:

I was 13 years old when we moved to Kenly, NC. We only lived one mile out of town so this was not too far for me to walk to the movie.

The home that we moved in did not even have an outhouse, enclosed privy. It was not uncommon not to have an outside privy at some of the Landlord's houses. Some time there would be a place behind the barn that you could sit on. This was before the Second World War and a short time after.

My Mom's Mom, Grandmom Carter would come and stay with us a week or two at a time and she remembered the way it was because having been born in 1869 she knew what it was like. We had a neighbor that also was a sharecropper living on the same landlord's farm. He told Dad that he called the Health Department and they made the landlord build an outhouse with a top, front door, and two holes inside. Dad contacted the Health Department and the landlord built us a new up dated outhouse. That was almost like having inside pluming now.

The old house was poorly constructed. It did not have any sheetrock on the walls inside the house The landlord told Dad if he would put up the sheetrock inside the house he would buy the materials to do it with, Dad agreed to this. The landlord told Dad that he had spent so much on the outhouse that he could not pay for the labor to install the sheetrock.

The house had a front porch and underneath the house was open to the wind chicken, dogs, cats, and anything that wanted to be under the house. The old floors had cracks that were wide enough to see chickens under the house.

Mom would buy some cheep linoleum to cover the floors. This would keep the wind out and keep the heat in. The house only had windows in the front. The doors were home-made, without door knobs. They had wood latches made into the door where it would hook in a slot. By lifting the latch it would open up the door.

The doors would let cold air in. During the summer we had to open the doors to let some air in. It was hard to keep out the flies and mosquitoes, we had no screen doors and without electric we could not have a fan. We cut wood for the fire place, cook stove, and wood heater in the living room. The old houses had only about 3 or 4 rooms.

The roof of a sharecropper's house was tin and it would rust. This would cause leaks all through the house. It was hard to sleep at night because of the heat. Most people sat out on the front porch and slapped mosquitoes until we went to bed. This was the way it was.

School:

When we moved to another farm, we would move during Christmas time. When school started back after Christmas that is when I would start to school at a new school. I became friends with a few boy and girls.

My friend told me that he had a little shoe shine box he carried every Saturday to town in Kenly, NC. This was how he made his money. He said that there was another boy shining shoes. I had already been to the movie theater but I had not noticed the shoe shine boys at that time.

I paid close attention to what he said. I knew if I wanted to go to the movies I had to make my own money or stay at home and listen to the radio or read a book. I told him at school I would see him in town on Saturday and that I wanted to see his shoe shine box.

I did not have any money for the movie so I asked Mom if I could take six eggs to town and sell them so I could go to the movies. She told me that she was saving all the good eggs because she had two hens that were to set and we needed the other eggs for breakfast. I only needed a quarter. I am not a thief, but when I left the house to go to town, I went by the chicken coop and took six eggs from the nest.

On that particular day the chickens had laid a few more eggs than usual. I took the eggs and put them in a little bag Mom kept in the hen house. The hen house was hidden from the house a little and Mom never missed the eggs. I never took anymore eggs after that.

I went to the Mom & Pop little grocery store with my eggs. He asked me how long had they been laid. I told him that they were laid today. The eggs would not last long without being in some type of cooler. He wanted to make certain that they were fresh. He gave me a dime for the eggs. I thought I would get more but that was the price.

I left and went to find my shoeshine buddy. I found him and watched him shine a pair of shoes. People did not line up to have their shoes shined. It was slow, but he made enough to have a little spending money. I watched him, and we talked for about an hour. During this time he shined three pairs of shoes at a dime each, this was 30 cents, big money. He showed me what he had in his box. He had two brushes one for brushing the shoes before he shined them and the other brush for shining. He had a popping rag that he could make it pop by jerking it fast and quick it would pop, he used both sides of the rag for a good shine. He had brown and black liquid and paste polish. He could make an old pair of shoes look new.

I told my friend I wanted to go to the movies but I only had a dime and I needed another nickel. He told me shining shoes was about over for the day but if I wanted to hang around and use his shoe shine box for a while I could. He told me where to hide the box when I was through.

He told me to hide it behind the theater in this certain bush so that when he came out he could find it. We were good friends and he trusted me. It wasn't long before two young guys walked up. One of them wanted a good shine all the way. All the way was to use both liquid and paste polish.

Step by step I did what my friend did and what he told me what to do. The guy was pleased with the job I did. This was a 15 cent shine. His buddy wanted his shoes shined but he said he only had a nickel left after paying his way in the movie, and buying a Pepsi and a box of popcorn. I needed that nickel real bad. I told him I would shine his shoes for that. With the 10 cents I got out of Mom's eggs and the 20 cents I made shining the shoes that gave me 30 cents, I was happy!

Shining Shoes:

The little shoe shine box was similar to a small carpentry tool box. It was about 14 inches long and 6 inches wide and about 12 inches tall. At the top the little flat board that you laid your foot on it was slanted downward a little toward the person. This made it easy for his foot to lay up there at a little drop down angle. It made it easy for the person to stand on one foot while shining his shoes. I would always shine shoes near or close to a building or pole so the person could hold to or lean on it.

More For His Money:

A person would get more for his money if he got his shoes shined with the liquid polish first and then I would wipe them down good with a soft cloth. Next I would use the paste wax. This would bring out the shine. It would bring 10 cents for this type of polish, but if he used 2 types of polish, I would get a nickel more, 15 cents for both polishes.

Between the first movie and the second movie there was a little comedy show. I hid the shoeshine box in the bushes like he told me and had enough money to pay my way in and had 6 cents left. I did not forget my Pepsi and popcorn.

My Own Shoe Shine Box:

The following week I found some boards that were left over from building the outhouse. This was enough to build my shoe shine box. In my mind I made my shoe shine box first the way my friend had his box. Side by side they looked the same size. I did a good job building it.

After building my rabbit boxes I had a little experience that made it easy to build my shoe shine box. All I had was a hammer, an old hand saw, and nails.

I told my Mom what I was doing, but she had already figured it out. She knew about the boys shining shoes uptown. I told my Mom all the things I needed for my shoe shine box. She said that her and Dad were going to town to sell three chickens and some eggs and that she would buy the things I needed. I was ready to shine shoes the very next Saturday.

When I got there on Saturday my friend saw me and told me the best place to get. You just could not put your shoe shine box anywhere. The way it was you had to put it where the most traffic was. Sometimes it could be an impulsive thing for the customer. If they saw you shining shoes they might decide to get theirs shined. Each person that wanted their shoes shined expected the shoe shine boy to be there.

Down about a block from where he was, close to the old General Store was a good place because the boy that was shining shoes there had moved with his family and he did good there.

I was proud of this because this was my first little business. I believe this was the beginning of my future years of self-employment. I shined 4 to 6 pairs of shoes every Saturday. Most of the time the same people would come by and I was building my customers

Just about everybody went to the movies because we had no TV and a lot of families did not have a radio. I really did good shining shoes. After shining shoes and hiding my box behind the theater, where my friend hid his box, I went to see the movie.

After the movies, I got my shoe shine box and walked across the street to the pool room. The movies were over at 11:00 p.m., but the pool room stayed open until 1:00 a.m. in the morning. I was happy that I could make my own money.

The pool room sold the best hot dogs and hamburgers that I have ever eaten. The price of a hot dog was 7 cents and a hamburger was a dime. The burger was a better buy. I had enough money to buy 2 hamburgers and a Pepsi and by that time of night I was hungry. The Pepsi Cola was at that time the most popular drink

At 13 years old I was already a business man, or thought I was. I was making my own money. After all this I had money left over to take to school. The school did not have a lunchroom. Most students carried their lunch. The school had this little concession room that a student could buy a drink to go with their lunch. The students could also buy a piece of candy and ice cream.

The students bought these things through this little window. The school did not have a ready-made dipped ice cream. All ice cream was frozen. I could buy this big drumstick ice cream cone. It was big, it had a big cone, and a lot of ice cream. The top was dipped in chocolate with nuts on top. I believe it would have weighed a half pound. It only cost a dime at school and away from school it was priced at 15 cents.

I do believe in the sixth, seventh, and eighth grades making my own money set me up for future years. As I got older, my feeling never changed. I learned by listening and watching other people and applying it to what I could do, I was a thinker.

I had another friend at the Kenly, NC school. He told me about trapping fur animals, minks, coons, opossum, and muskrats. He told me that he went with his Dad checking his traps on their trap line.

I listened real good because I thought that was something I could do. I started saving my money, as much as I could because I knew I had to have money to buy my steel traps with.

The trapping season came in the fall of the year and stayed in through the winter months. I saved all the money I could through the summer months by barning tobacco, picking cotton, and shining shoes. This gave me enough time to save enough money to buy my three steel traps.

At the end of the crop season I went to the old General Store to look at the steel traps. They had different kinds of steel traps. One for just about anything you wanted to catch; fox, mink, otters, opossum, coons, and muskrats. I told the sell's person what type of traps I needed, that I was only catching muskrats. I told him about the small canal behind our house going through the corn field from the big branch down in the woods.

I told him that we had lots of muskrats up and down that ditch because I could see the holes and signs on the side of the banks where they would come in and out of the water from the top of the water up to the bank where their den holes were and slick because of their travel.

He said you should be able to catch a lot of muskrats but hide these new traps with grass on top of them. This would help them blend in with the area.

I asked him which ones are the best for the muskrats and he showed me the best ones for them. They had all kinds of traps some big ones, and some with springs in them to fall larger animals. He told me I only needed a small trap because a muskrat wasn't a big animal and the trap would not break his leg off, but would be strong enough to hold him.

The war had not been over for only a few years and everything made of steel was expensive. The best that I can remember, I paid about $9.00 for three muskrat traps. This was big money. The average person would never have this much money at one time, but I had saved up for this. He was surprised that I had $9.00.

I found out when the season came in from my friend and that his father trapped the big branch of water in the woods and they would not trap my small canal because they did not get on anybody's farm to trap.

I asked him where could I sell my furs and he told me how to prepare the muskrats for sell after I caught them. He said when his Dad sold his furs, he would sell my furs.

Skinning my Animals:

My friend told me how to skin them and let them dry before I could sell them because the fur buyer would not buy them if the skins are not dried out good. He said that I had to make a little flat board and after skinning my muskrat, the fur would be inside out. He told me to be careful skinning them and stretching the fur on the little board because if I cut or tear a hole in the fur, that it would not bring as much money.

I was OK with this because I skinned the rabbits I caught in my rabbit boxes and I knew what to do. He said a muskrat was harder to skin than a rabbit and he explained to me how he and his Dad skinned theirs. They would tack the hind feet with a nail to a post or tree and start at the back legs and work the fur down all the way to the head all in one piece. It had to be the whole skin. When I got to the head, it would take time skinning around the eyes, ears, and mouth. As I skinned the muskrat, cutting a little at a time and pulling the skin down as I cut, it all came out good. This was slow work because you did not want to cut a hole in the fur. In the 30's and 40's fur business was a good business.

Catching Muskrats:

In the fall when the trapping season came in, I found some good muskrat holes and slides. They would have their den just above the top of the water. I could find them easy. It took good skills to catch a muskrat, but they were not a smart as a mink. I would look for the best holes and slides on the bank of the little creek.

All fur animals that live in rivers, creeks, and marshes depend on water ways for catching their food. They build their dens a little above the water level in the rivers and creeks. The reason for this is if the river or creek water comes up in their holes, it won't be high enough to drown their babies because they could not swim at this age.

My friend told me I would need a rifle to shoot them in the head because they would eat you up if they could. I had to make sure I shot them in the head so that I would not mess up the fur.

I went to the Old General Store and purchased a single shot 22 rifle and I managed to pay for it from my shoe shine money. It cost a lot of money, this was in 1948, I paid $4.50 for it.

I had only three traps, so I had to make the best of it. Setting traps was not an easy job they had to be just right. I would use bailing (small wire) to tie to the trap and tie the other end of the wire to a big root or bush. If I had neither, I would stab a tobacco stick deeply in the ground. I tried to find a place near the den so when the muskrat got caught and tried to get free he would fall in the water and drown with the trap attached to him.

Sometimes I set my traps at the water level where his slide slick would go in the water or I would set it at the mouth of his den hole if I had enough room. I would pull up some dead grass around it and lay the grass on top of the trap to hide it.

Until the traps got rusty a little they were too shinny and would not catch anything. Camouflaging the traps was the best way all the time. I did good catching them because there were a lot of them. I skinned and prepared them just like my friend told me.

Selling my Furs:

My friend's Dad had furs to sell just about every week during trapping season. He made lots of money because he was catching minks, weasels, coons, opossums, and some muskrats through the woods on that creek. The creek ran for miles. When I had my muskrats ready his Dad would sell them and that was good money. The fur business was good.

My friend did not live far away from me. I would ride my bicycle to his house when I had any furs to sale. Times were hard and there was not much money. My friend's Dad sold my furs for $1.75 each. He would sale them to a fur buyer in Wilson, NC about 15 miles away. I learned that they would sell all their furs to the Hudson Bay Fur Company in New York, the largest fur company in the USA.

This was more money than I could make helping sharecroppers in the late fall. The muskrats were a dark fur animal and it looked like a big barn rat except for its tail. With shining shoes and catching muskrats that winter I made a lot of money. I would buy good clothes and wear pretty shoes. I had money to spend and all the little girls at school were beginning to notice me. I was a poor sharecropper's son but I was in there with the elite.

During the first winter I trapped and shined shoes and with my single shot 22 Rifle I went squirrel hunting. That season I killed 83 squirrels and with 3 rabbit boxes setting I caught 57 rabbits. We could not eat all of them so, I gave our neighbors squirrels and rabbits all winter. There was a little Mom & Pop Store in town and he would buy rabbits from me, but I would have to leave a non-skinned foot on each rabbit so people would know that it was a rabbit and not a cat.

The Mom & Pop Store bought them on Saturday early in the morning. Without electric I had to keep them on ice. He only would buy what I caught on Friday and Saturday. I would take the rabbits out of the boxes early every morning. It could be from 2 to 6 rabbits that he would buy. He paid me 50 cents each for them. The store would sell them for $1.00 each. Most of the town had electric but it had not been installed through the county.

By the time I was fourteen I started growing up a little. My voice started changing to a ruff type sounding voice. I had dark black wavy hair and a lot of little girls began to pay attention to me.

Almost every Saturday night I would make a date with one to meet me at the movies. If I had enough money I would pay their way in the movie, if I didn't they would pay their own way in. Sometimes they would have to wait for me to finish shining shoes and sometimes I would find them in the movie and would set beside them and we could hold hands. After the movie, I would get my shoe shine box from the bushes and go to the pool room. Fred Floors Pool Room stayed opened until 1:00 in the morning.

I was making big money and had enough to buy a hamburger and a Pepsi. The Pepsi was the most popular drink back then. A hot dog was 7 cents and a hamburger was a dime. They made the best burger you could find anywhere.

Figure 1 – Soy Bean Field

Figure 2 A mare horse that can mate with a
male donkey can produce a mule.

Figure 3 – A soy bean field with an old tobacco barn in the back of the field.

Figure 4 – A cotton field

Figure 5 – An old sharecropper's house

Figure 6 – An old log tobacco barn that would cure tobacco with wood.

Figure 7 – Another old sharecropper's house.

Figure 8 – A tobacco field.

Figure 9 – A corn field.

Figure 10- A two horse mowing machine for cutting hay.

Figure 11- A one horse corn and cotton planter..

Figure 12 – A one mule hay rake for easy harvesting of hay.

Figure 13 – A two mule tobacco transplanter with two seats at the back and up front is a big water drum to water each plant that is set out and the driver has a seat on top of the water drum.

Figure 14 – A two mule stalk cutter, in the center is the blades as the mule pulls that go around and cut the stalks of corn and tobacco. There is a driver's seat on top.

Figure 15 – A two mule cultivator with a driver's seat and left of seat is a fertilizer distributor, beneath the seat are several little plows.

Figure 16 – a two mule hay rake for harvesting hay.

Figure 17 – A hay field.

Figure 18 – An old tobacco barn with a wrap around shelter to hang the green tobacco and work under while it is raining.

Figure 19 – This is a much newer tobacco barn with a larger wrap around shelter that also was used for farm equipment.

Figure 13 1928 Model T Ford

Figure 29 The house before the deck below was built

Figure 31 Removing the intestines

Figure 34 This was a pig cooking contest

Figure 35 Judging the BBQ pigs

Figure 36 Some pig cookers the Author built

Figure 37 Cooking contest

Figure 38 BBQ chopping board that the Author made

Figure 45 Display of foil print pictures - rack jobbing over 200 accounts including some WalMart stores for five years

Figure 46 My warehouse and trucks being used in my panty hose rack jobbing business for thirteen years

**Figure 47 My last business - hot dog cart on
Camp Lejeune Base for two years**

I Became an Entrepreneur:

The second winter I did the same thing, setting traps for muskrats. This winter was like the one before, things had not changed much.

I turned 15 years old on December 2, 1950. I can recall where I bought a gold looking pocket watch with a long gold chain attached to it. In the early years pants were made for boys and men with a pocket watch pocket right above the right side pocket. My gold chain hung down to my knees. Boy I was in there with the rich kids. Not many kids had a gold pocket watch with a long chain.

That winter about the end of February we moved again to the Selma area, about six miles away from Kenly, NC. In the sixth and seventh grades living at Kenly was the best two years of my life. Now things will change fast for me. Living in Kenly was when I started being my own self, have my own thoughts, and be my own man. My feelings never changed from that time on.

I learned by listening, watching other people, and applying it for what I thought would be best for me. I became a smart kid. I knew then and there if I wanted anything I had to work for it.

Saving my Money:

That last year living in Kenly, my brother Roy and my sister Laura left home. Roy went to Claremont, NC, near the mountain area to live with Uncle Albert. This was our

Uncle that was in the war. He was employed with a furniture factory making furniture of all kinds. So it was easy for Roy to get a job.

Shortly after Roy left, Laura got married to a well-to-do outstanding young man and in less than a year, he joined the Air Force to keep from going to the Army. They moved to Texas that fall after all the crops were harvested.

After moving to Selma, I knew I had to get a job. I helped every sharecropper that I could. In the spring, by doing everything and preparing their fields along with our farm, I made a little money. I was not broke by a long shot because I had saved my money at Kenly. I knew I would need a car before long.

When tobacco barning season came, my Mom, Dad, and myself had to swap labor for barning tobacco. Wages went up a little that year. Croppers got one dollar per hour and barn help got 50 cents per hour. I had to be a cropper that year and this would pay more.

Back to My Driver's License:

When I was 14 I started thinking about a car. It would only be 2 more years before I could drive. Back then they had no driver's education classes. You learned by driving up and down dirt roads and paths, if you even had a car to practice with.

I drove my Dad's old 37 Chevrolet Coupe on dirt roads and in the country. That was about all the driving I had with a car. When I became sixteen I told Dad I wanted to get my driver's license. He told me I wasn't ready yet and I asked him what I needed to do to be ready, a little more time and a little older.

That's like telling me not to go down to the river with the boys until I learned how to swim, well how will I learn how to swim if I don't get in the water? I finally convinced him to let me take my driver's test with Uncle Tommy's new 1952 Chevrolet because I did not want to take the test on that old 37 Chevrolet Coupe because the steering wheel was so loose I could hardly hold it in the road.

My Uncle Tommy agreed that I could. My Dad, Uncle Tommy, and I went to the town of Goldsboro. I passed the written test and next was the driving test. The patrolman asked me had I ever driven this car. I told him I had not, that it was my Uncle's car. He said this looked like a new car. I told him it was and I was afraid to drive it. I had never driven a car in town before. I was scared to death!!

We sat in the car and he told me where to go, right in the heart of down town Goldsboro, NC! I was on the edge of my seat. We came back to the Patrol Station and he told my Uncle Tommy and my Dad not to let me drive by myself until I had learned to drive with more experience. I got my driver's license. That was the way it was back then, compared to how they learn to drive now before they get their license.

I had a cousin that bought his first car at 18 years of age. He was a go getter type of person. He stopped school when he was 15 and got a job off the farm and made his own money. I wanted to do the same.

I did not want to drive Dad's old 1937 Chevrolet Coupe. I helped everybody in the neighborhood that I could to make all the money I could. I knew if I did not buy my own car, I would not have any way to travel and find a job or help people in my area near home.

I needed to buy a car and to buy one fast. So the quicker I bought myself a car, the quicker I could get more jobs. People wanted you to be dependable because back then it was real important to get to work on time. The more I worked, the more money I would have.

I worked everyday doing something. The three of us swapped help or work with our new neighbors. What time I was not swapping work barning tobacco with our neighbors, I was working with some of the local sharecroppers doing whatever they had me to do, I had to make my own money because swapping work, you did not get paid, that would come at the end of barning tobacco season

When school started back in the fall I knew I had to get out of the house and find me a part-time job. I had just got my driver's license and I was 16 years old almost 17.

Dad had an old 37 Chevrolet Coup. He would let me drive the car just a little. This helped me to find a part-time job. The nearest town was Selma, about 3 miles from where we lived. I took the old 37 Chevy Coup and went to Selma on a Saturday. This new grocery store had just opened up in Selma and that was the first place I went. It was owned by Vernon Wiggs and his wife.

I talked to him and he wanted to know what I could do. I started telling him how I made my own money and before I got through he told me to come next Friday after school and work until closing and all day on Saturday. He wanted to know could he depend on me because he would need me every weekend, he was closed on Sunday. I told him that I was saving my money to buy me a car and that I would be dependable.

This was a good looking new super market. He had a meat department and a big vegetable bin down one side of the store. Mr. Wiggs had everything that you needed. There were lots of customers trading with him. This was a long ways up from the Old General Store and the small Mom's & Pop's Stores. Of course they were still in business. But a lot of things began to change in a hurry and some of the Mom's and Pop's stores were becoming new stores like Mr. Wiggs'.

Mr. Wiggs's store was the only super market in the town of Selma. A few miles away was a town called Smithfield and it had an A & P Super Market. My jobs in the store was learn to do everything, except use the cash register. This was fast work but easy to learn and when to do it. I played a big part in doing things.

I had to count eggs to be traded for groceries. The price for young pullet eggs or a young chicken just beginning to lay eggs was different, I had to sort them out because there were all mixed up. I wrote down on a little card the number of eggs that the customer brought in and the amount we owed them. I would hand the cards to the cashier with their name on it and what we owed them.

When the customer came up with their groceries the cashier would ring them up and if they had brought in eggs, she would deduct the price of the eggs from their purchase and the customer paid the difference.

Another one of my jobs was working back in the vegetable area, weighing, bagging vegetables, and writing the price on the bag of what it was and the price of it. The scales did not give you the price, so most of the time I would round everything off at the pound numbers. The price of the vegetables had a price in front of each vegetable.

Mr. Wiggs only had 5 people working in the store, two men in the meat department, the cashier, Mr. Wiggs, and myself. His wife would come in on the weekend to run another register. I loved my job, it was fast work and I was making my money. He paid me 35 cents an hour, the cashier was only making 45 cents an hour. We closed up at 9:00 pm. on Saturday night and opened up at 6:00 a.m. The super market was on 301 Highway where it could be seen good. It had a big sign out front.

By the time I boxed up all the vegetables and put them away in the cooler, what needed to be in the cooler, it was getting late. I had to wash down the vegetable bins and clean them good. It was about 10:00 p.m. time to lock up and leave.

Sometime during the closing time he would pay me. He would pay me from 6 am to 10 at night. I had a 30 minute lunch hour but he would pay me for that. I made 16 hours on Saturday. I worked from 4 p.m. to 10 pm on Friday, this would be 6 hours total. This would give me 22 hours and 22 hours times 35 cents was $7.70, this was big money.

Dad let me drive the old 37 Chevrolet Coupe. In order to drive the car, Dad wanted me to put $2.00 worth of gas in it that would almost fill it up. The gas was only 22 cents per gallon. After leaving the super market, I drove about 3 blocks where the pool room was to buy me a hamburger. They had gone up to fifteen cents and I could buy a drink and two hotdogs for thirty cents.

The pool room in Selma and in Kenly had the best burgers and dogs anywhere. The only ingredients that came on a hot dog were onions, chili, mustard, and you put the ketchup on it if you wanted it.

I worked for Mr. Wiggs for two years and I learned a lot. The location is still in business today which is an old IGA Supermarket.

My Soybean Field:

The last two years in high school, Dad gave me a 5 acre field to plant soybeans for my hogs. I knew I had to make the best of this because this is the last chance I would have I had to make this work. I had grown up a lot and was a good thinker, I could see my future.

When we left Kenly and moved to the Selma area, Dad had bought a 2 mule riding plow. This made plowing easy because I could ride while plowing and not walk behind the plow. This year as we started farming, I found out our neighbor had a 2 mule riding cultivator that he wanted to sell because he had bought him a little Red Tractor to farm with. I knew I had to do most of the cultivating on the farm and I asked him would he sell it to me. He said he would if I had any money.

He was surprised that I had the money to pay for it. He said he would take $20.00 for it and all the plow shoes that went with it. I bought it and was happy I had another farm equipment that I could ride on.

It had a fertilizer distributor that would dispense the amount of fertilizer you wanted to go to the row that you were planting or while cultivating. It also had a seed planter attached to it and that would make it easy, because I did not have to walk behind the one horse seed planter.

Between jobs on the farm and working with my neighbors every chance I could to make what money I could. I would plow and disk my soybean field between jobs until I got through with it and it was ready to plant. With that two mule cultivator it would not take long to plant the beans.

While going to school and before school was out for the summer, after school was out for the day, just about every evening I would help neighbors until dark.

When I planted my soybean field I bought good hybrid soybeans. I wanted my bean field to grow big and produce a lot of beans. This was in the early 50's and a lot of people had tractors. Farming was getting a lot better with less work as time went on, it didn't happen overnight. It took a few years before farming was any easier to do.

When I planted my soybeans, I did not put any fertilizer to my beans. Soybeans did not require much fertilizer because they would get a lot of nourishment from the ground and air. The soybeans would build up the soil in the ground and make the field richer for the next year's planting. After the beans came up and got about a foot tall, I would cultivate them and at the same time I would fertilize them while cultivating the field. It didn't take much fertilizer for the beans. This would be the last time I would cultivate my soybean field.

Buying Pigs:

When it was time to barn tobacco this year I was ready to make all the money I could and buy some pigs for my bean field. I had three pigs at this time. I worked with other sharecroppers every day I could.

After swapping with other farmers in the area, I had two days a week to help others. But on Friday evening and Saturday I had to work at the super market.

Mr. Wall lived in the area and he wanted me to help him with his tobacco. I heard him talking in the field that he had a sow with eight pigs and in two or more weeks they would be big enough to wean (taken from the sow). I was excited. I needed those pigs. I thought about the pigs until we barned tobacco the next week. So then I asked him if he would sell me the pigs. He was surprised that I asked. I told him I wanted them when they got weaned. I was going to buy me a car.

Mr. Wall told me he would. He asked me how are you going to pay for them. I told him I could give him $30.00 now and he could keep my pay and not pay me and let that help pay for the rest of the pigs. He said alright we will do it that way. I gave him the $30.00 and he told me by the time I picked the pigs up at the end of six weeks of barning tobacco, now at this time they will be eight weeks old and would be a lot bigger than at six weeks at weaning age. I believed he felt sorry for me and wanted to help me.

I made eight dollars a day with him. At the end of the barning tobacco season, Mr. Wall told me I could get the pigs with the $30.00 I had paid him and the $30.00 more I paid him total of $60.00 for the eight pigs. I had a little money left helping him barn tobacco. He kept the pigs 2 weeks longer than six weeks. Boy they had really gotten big except there was a runt in the bunch (a runt is a lot smaller than the others).

By keeping them 2 weeks longer, I asked him how much more did I owe him, he said we would call it even since there was a runt in the bunch. I really got a deal because being 8 weeks old they would eat more and get larger quicker. He brought them over, we put them in my pen with my other three that I had. My bean field was not ready yet to put the hogs in there. It would be only a week or two before the beans were ready. They had pads hanging on the stalks about but had to fill out with beans inside them, first came beautiful flowers and then the pads.

Fencing the Bean Field with Electric Wire:

We had electric at this farm. In order to keep the hogs in the bean field, Dad and I had to string an electric wire around the whole field. This took a lot of wire and wire insulators.

The insulators were of porcelain and round with a hole in the center for the number size 10 nail and they were white in color. I had a little money left from buying the pigs. I was a stingy little fellow, I had to be I didn't make money every day.

I went to the Old General Store to buy the wire and the electric control voltage control box. This was the same store in Pine Level that we purchased just about everything.

Dad and I had walked the field to know how much wire to buy. Dad had long legs and his average steps were 36 inches, one yard apart. So we kept up with the steps and that would tell us how many feet of wire to buy. We purchased what we needed. We used tobacco sticks cut in half for the insulators. We knew how many sticks we would need at a distance of 20 feet apart. We nailed the insulators on the sticks first and alow the tobacco sticks (stakes) how far to put them in the ground and have the wire tied to the insulators 10 inches from the ground. First we staked the sticks in the ground and it took lots and lots of them. We took bailing wire to tie the electric wire on the insulator. We made sure that we cleaned out from under the wire and around it. If anything touched the wire it would short out the electric box. At the entrance or gate we had a long electric cord running to the tobacco barn for our current.

I had to make some watering troughs because hogs would drink a lot of water. I had to do this before I put the pigs in the field. This is how I made them. I took 2 x 10 eight foot boards and nailed them together so they would make a V. It required 2 of them. Then at each end I cut an 8 x 10 board half way and this gave me 2 each 4 foot pieces for two troughs. I then nailed one piece at each in of the trough. I would pour water in the trough to let it swell up so it would not leak once I put the pigs in the pasture.

Each end of the trough was 4 feet, this would be hard for the pigs to root under it and turn it over. A hog's nature is to root and this would be the first thing that they would do to root and see if they could find something under the watering troughs. The troughs would be wide at the top and would look like a V shape.

To make things better for the bean field and around the watering troughs, we put hog rings in all the pig's snouts to keep them from rooting up the bean field and rooting around the watering troughs.

Dad would hold the pig by the ears and between his legs with the front feet off the ground. I would take the nose ringer and put about three rings in their nose. This would hurt if they tried to root. A few hogs could root and tear up a whole farm if they ran loose. (A ringer is a clamp that is big and it is clamped through the hog's nose.)

You must keep water in them all the time because if they dried out the boards would shrink and they would not hold water until you gave them a few days to swell up again. These troughs could be used for mules, cows, goats, chickens, and just about any animal. They also would be good for feeding animals. They are good for shelled corn, beans, dry foods, slops, or just about anything.

The Soybean Bush:

The soybean bushes grew to about 2 to 3 feet high. They would produce blooms near the center of the stalks. The blossoms would be different colors and they were beautiful.

Each bloom would grow into a pod and each pod would have about six to eight beans in them. When the pods became big and the beans inside were filled out that was the time we put the pigs in the bean field.

The beans would stay green a long time until cold weather turned them brown. We could not see the little pigs once we put them in the field. Mostly during the evening when they came to the troughs to drink water, we could see that we had all of them and none had gotten out under the wire. The pigs would eat the leaves and beans. The fresh leaves help make them fat.

As time went on you could see a skeleton of a bean stalk where they had eaten everything from the stalk. We also gave them a little supplement, this was a grind up mixture of corn, beans, wheat, and with minerals added, it would make them healthy and fat.

Occasionally we would give the hogs along with some slops from the house with some of Mom's lye soap mixed in with the slops to kill hook worms. Just like today commercial hog farmers give hogs some type of mineral to kill the worms

A hog is one of the smartest animals. If they came close to the wire, they would know that something was wrong. They would sniff the wire and back off. But if they did not see the wire and touched it with their ears, they would receive an electric shock and back off. They would not hit it again. They would always look for it being there.

A Second Litter of Pigs:

As luck would have it, I met one of Mr. Wigg's customers one Saturday his name was Ralph Brown. We were talking in general about farming. I mentioned to him that I had a field of soybeans with electric wire running around it for my hogs and after they ate up most of the beans I was going to sell them to buy a car.

Then he said that he had a litter of nine pigs that he took from the sow (weaned) two weeks ago, they were eating good, and he need to sell them now. He said that he was going to breed the sow and have another litter of pigs. A sow has two litters of pigs a year. It takes about 3 months, 3 weeks, and 3 days for her gestation period (114 days).

Mr. Ralph Brown had come in the super market before and I knew who he was. I asked him if he did not have to sell them now that I needed some more pigs in my bean field. The soybeans were almost filled out to put the hogs in the field now. I was thinking this would make a total of 20 pigs and I needed them. I told him I could not buy them, I had no money. I said in about three months they would be ready to sell and they would grow fast and whatever his pigs brought that we would split the money in half.

He liked the idea and asked me where I lived. He said he would ride by and look at my bean field. He came back to the store and said that the field was a good crop of beans. If I would keep them for three months that he would bring them to the field. I said that this is fine with me. In about two days he brought them over. Every so often he would go by and look at them. He was ok with the way they were putting on weight.

I was trying to get my ducks in a row. I did not have much time before I got out of high school. I only had two more years or less. Along with my pigs and working in the super market I was determined to drive a bus.

I asked Mr. Batten, principal of Micro, NC school could I take the school bus driving course. He said I could and if I did not get a bus I could make a substitute driver for the other drivers. I did not want to do this. I wanted my own bus. I knew right then if I got a bus in the 11th grade I had to be good because not many students in the 11th grade drove a school bus.

My School Bus:

I tried out that summer. All during the training course I watched the older students and I came to notice that I was just as good as the rest of them. I could tell that the instructor liked the way I drove and the understanding of the bus. I passed the course with flying colors and I knew I had done a good job. I had not heard anything until Mr. Batten came to our old farm house about a week before school. It started back in September. He said that he would come back tomorrow and drive me throughout my bus route.

Back then it was dirt roads, except getting on 301 for a short distance to the school house. You might remember at the beginning of this book, I started in the first grade at Micro living near the railroad tracks and often moving around all over the county and now I am finishing high school at Micro.

Back when I started to work my job at Vernon Wiggs' Super Market where we moved to, I could have gone to Pine Level, Selma, or Micro. I started at Micro in the first grade so I decided to finish there. I am glad I did. Everything worked out good. This was a long route. It was all dirt roads and through the county and I had to cross two railroad tracks.

This was the longest route that we had and slow driving because all the roads were so bad. Back then the county had these big road scrappers to go up and down the road knocking down the bumps and filling in the holes, making the road smooth but this did not last long. The roads rode good for a few days. After each rain it was right back the way they were, bumpy with holes. The bus would only go 40 mph because it had a governor build in the motor to control the speed. Most of the time on those bumpy roads you could not go 40 mph.

Each month the bus drivers got their checks from the state for driving the bus for the nine months of the school year. This was big money. The bus drivers received $22.00 per month. This was a lot of money compared to how much you got paid barning tobacco or picking cotton.

After the 11th grade that year before the 12th grade, I had to take the bus training course again to drive in the 12th grade. I found out during this training course after last year's training course, Mr. Batten asked the instructor who were the best students for driving a bus. He told Mr. Batten that I was one of the best.

When school started back in the 12th grade, Mr. Batten gave me the 301 route, because of my experience with driving in the 11th grade. This was the first big responsibility of my life. I realized in the 11th grade that if I drove in the 12th grade I had to do a good job.

Back in the 11th grade when school started this mother that worked in the school lunch room, she and her two little girls, one in the first and the other in the third, they rode on my bus. Mr. Batten reserved the first seat right behind the driver's seat for her and her two little girls. This would be better sitting in the first seat for the three of them because they would not have walk up and down the bus looking for a seat.

After a few weeks she told Mr. Batten that I was one of the best drivers that she had ever seen. Her name was Mrs. Parrish and her husband was a farmer. She rode the bus the nine months of that school year. The price for lunch at school was 25 cents and ½ pint of milk was 4 cents if you wanted an extra ½ pint.

Hazel the Hurricane:

On October 15, 1954, Hazel came through North Carolina. Johnston County was a direct hit. The Hurricane made landfall between North Carolina's and South Carolina's border near Calabash North Carolina.

This was the first category four Hurricane on record to hit North Carolina and the worst. The storm killed over 400 people in Haiti, 95 people in the US before going all the way through Canada near Toronto and killing 81 more people. The top winds were recorded at 140 miles per hour when it hit the US.

It came through the Johnston County area destroying outhouses, lots of trees, and most of all the bushy type Chainey Ball trees. During the storm most farmers quoted that they saw their outhouse and the Chainey Ball trees going across the field, flipping over and over one right behind the other one.

It also blew down light poles. They could be seen up and down the dirt roads and throughout some of the fields.

On this day, October 15, 1954, at 6 a.m. Hazel came offshore and by the time school opened up that morning at 8:00 a.m. the winds began to blow. Most of us did not know that we had a Hurricane.

Mr. Batten found out a little late that morning. By the time we all got to school and into our classes, Mr. Batten announced over the speaker that school was letting out and for everyone to get to their bus immediately because the Hurricane was about to hit us and if we all left now we would get home in time before the eye hit.

The News:

Back then the news was slow and a lot of people did not have a TV, mostly radio news. The wind was blowing hard at this time. The buses were loading up and it took only about 10 minutes to load all the buses. All total from about 8:00 until the buses pulled out to go home about 15 minutes had passed. Lots of the kids were getting scared. I had to quiet them down on the bus they were getting out of hand. They were good kids they just got scared. I assured them that we all should make it home before the storm hit us bad.

This was my first big storm that I had seen and none of the kids on the bus had seen a big one like this before. I pulled out of the school yard and the wind was picking up a little at a time. I had to go down north on 301 about 2 miles and then cross the railroad tracks. About 2 more miles my first student would get off. It started to rain hard by that time. It was hard driving because of the wind and rain. I had 52 students on the bus when I left school that morning. The school buses back then were short. It was full with 52 students aboard. Each bus back then had a door person that would open and close the door and help the little ones in the bus. John was a good friend of mine. We both were in the 11th grade and he did a good job.

Gradually the wind was picking up as we let the students out at their homes. The bus was shaking and the rain got worse. I told John that I hope that I could finish the route before it got much worse.

It didn't take long before the eye hit us. The road was slick and by this time it was hard to see where I was going. The dirt roads had a clay dirt-looking top and this made it even worse to keep the bus in the road. I could feel the bus sliding a little and not stopping as quick when I put on brakes.

Sometimes the wind was so hard we could not open the door all that good. By this time we had most of the students off the bus. I could see that the parents were helping their kids in the house.

Detouring:

The roads were wet and slippery. I could see that the wind had blown down the electric poles alongside the road and some in the fields. I absolutely could not go fast. The wind was blowing into the bus and it held me back to a slow speed. I was just creeping along and before I knew what was happening, it blew my bus in the road ditch and out of the ditch. I did not have much control of the bus. We did not have deep roadside ditches and the bus being high up from the ground we did not get stuck.

By that time I was scared but no one on the bus knew it. I only had to get these kids home. I only had seven kids left on the bus.

Power Lines:

Up ahead a little ways around a little curve I saw the electric lines laying in and across the road, both poles had fallen down one on each side of the road. The wire was live with fire. I could see sparks from them on the road. I had to make a decision and I set there thinking my only chance I had was to turn the bus around in the middle of the road. I knew that it had to be done. This was the way they taught me during the driving test we took. But this road was narrow. My only hope was to turn it around. So I drove up close to the ditch and backed up about 5 or 6 feet at a time. It took about 8 to 10 backing and pulling up until I had the bus pointed back the other way. The Lord was with us because it could have turned up side down.

All of us were so scared we could not speak a word. I thought how will I do this; getting them home. I decided the best way was to go to the end of my route and put the seven students off that way.

The wind did not let up, it got worse driving to the end of my route and until I got everybody off the bus. It felt like the bus at sometimes was up on its side and back down on the road and up again. After it was all over I knew I made the right decision by reversing my route. I can recall these two little boys next to the last stop getting off the bus. They got to the porch and on the porch a gust of wind came and blew them off the porch down at the end and on the ground. I waited and saw their dad come out and help them in the house. Then I drove off and had one more little girl on the bus. Her mom opened the front door and helped her get in the house.

I had to make some more detours to get back on the right road and back on the paved Highway 301. Then on the way home I went.

I had to drive about 5 miles to get home. The storm did not let up it was bad. I made it and when I drove in the yard, Mom was looking out the window for me to show up. Mom was glad that I was home and no one got hurt.

I still think of that Hurricane from time to time and to this day I can't believe I got through it without the school bus getting stuck or the bus turned on its side.

When we went back to school the next Monday I told Mr. Batten the principal about how I got the students home. How I had to detour because of the electric lines across the road. He thanked me for my ways of handling all that and he was proud of me.

Selling my Hogs:

After about three months the pigs ate just about all the beans and what they did not eat we cut down for hay. I told Mr. Ralph Brown that the three months were up and I was going to sell my pigs. He came over to look at them and he told me that there were pretty. He would take 4 of the nine that I started with and put them in his pen for hog killing. They all were about the same size and I told him if he took four that he can have the four biggest ones. He was happy because the pigs were the right size to sell for the best money per pound.

At six to eight weeks at weaning the pigs will weigh about 50 pounds each after three months his four pigs each will weigh close to 175 to 180 pounds. They would be called top hogs this weight will bring the most per pound. I left my sixteen in the field a few days longer to put on all the weight they could while I looked for me a car at the going price. I could figure just about how much money I would receive from them at the auction sale. So I started looking for a car. I will only sell 12 and leave the others for hog killing.

My Car:

It did not take long before I found a pretty sky blue 49 Ford 8 cyl. Flat head engine and it was clean. This used car dealer in the little town of Pine Level, NC had the car, his name was Fred. I told him I had some hogs I was going to sell if he would keep it for a day or two until I sold them. He had told me he wanted $400.00 for the car and would not take any less. I agreed to buy it.

He wanted $20.00 to hold the car for me. That was almost all the money I had. I sold the pigs in Wilson at the hog auction. I knew that the hogs would not bring that much, but I was going to get that car some way. My pigs brought me after paying auction fees $309.00. I had planned all along what I was going to do about borrowing the rest of the money

I took the pigs' money and went to the Old General Store where we bought most of our food and other things with the coupon book that we got once a month. I told Mr. Bee

Oliver, the owner, that I wanted to buy a 49 Ford from Fred and I needed about $100.00 more after telling him what I received from the pigs.

Mr. Oliver knew my Dad because we traded with him with those coupon books. He asked me, "how will you pay it back?". I told him that I was driving a school bus and had a job with Vernon Wiggs' Supper Market in Selma. That really impressed him. I told him that I would pay it back $10.00 per month or more if I could.

I told Mr. Oliver that Dad's old 37 Chevrolet Coupe would not last and I was afraid that it would give out anytime. I did not want that to happen coming home so late at night. He agreed to lend me the money. He took the money out of his pocket and gave it to me. He would not keep any record with his bookkeeper and when I paid each month just give him the money.

Within 5 months I had Mr. Bee Oliver paid up. It was not mandatory for me to have insurance on the car. A lot of people had insurance on their car. This was the year 1954, the year that Hazel (the Hurricane) came through NC.

Within only a few years, in the last of the 50's, the state made everyone carry insurance on their car, truck, and bus.

In the early 50's there were thousands of vehicles on the roads in the state of NC without insurance. I cannot help but think back to those days why did it take North Carolina so long for this to be mandatory. The highway patrolmen were more enforced and they would get you for speeding with a wire trap across the road.

Out of High School:

After finishing high school, I married my high school sweetheart. We both were young. She was 19 and I was 20. I left my 49 Ford at home for my Dad and I bought a good used one owner 1950 Chevrolet, low mileage from a good neighbor Mr. Herman Brown.

My wife and I moved to Raleigh. She got a job with the Revenue Department. I got a job with the Great Atlantic and Pacific Tea Com. (A & P). I worked at their supply warehouse out on the Wake Forest Road. This was night work. My job was loading trucks along with 11 more employees. Everything That the A & P Super Markets sold is what was loaded in those big 18 wheeler trucks.

The A & P had a lot of locations throughout the Carolinas. A & P did not own their own trucks. The big trucks were owned by Boone Trucking Company. Trucking had come a long way in the 50's. They were bigger and could carry up to 50,000 pounds.

At night we would have 9 – 12 fellows in the warehouse getting up the food supplies. The men inside the trucks would load the trucks, according to what they had to load. The warehouse fellows along with me used these small low flat 4 wheelers that we could push easy to the back of the big trucks that were backed up at the loading dock.

I can remember this being hard work. We had to load about 10 big trucks at night and it would take time and a lot to fill them up. We would start to work about 6:00 p.m. and finish about 3:00 to 4:00 a.m. We would take a 30 minute break at 12:00 each night and being a bunch of men and young boys like myself you can just imagine things what we talked about during the break period.

There were two brothers that worked there and had been there a few years before I came to work with A & P. Both had been in the Army. They were not old, about 30 or 35 years of age. I will never forget them. They both had red hair, freckles, and their last name was Hilderbrand. I can't recall their first name. I got acquainted with them good. I can recall a tall black young man in his mid 20's and his name was Bumchauis. I never did find out his first or last name. He was a funny character.

We had a couple of bigger guys over two hundred pounds all doing the same job I was doing. The Hildrebrand boys talked about being in the military, that they were tough and strong. So I got tired of hearing them brag about all they had done. I said to them so you think you are strong if so, go to that one hundred pound bag of potatoes and lift a bag over your head.

They said the hell, that no one in here could do it. I thought I could if I could get my hands under it just right because it had to lay flat on the palm of both hands just right so it would not roll off. I was 21 years old and only weighed 160 pounds and 5'11" tall. Keep in mind I was the second smallest person there. I said to them, do I have any bets that I can't lift that bag of potatoes over my head. One said I'll bet $5.00, the other said $10.00, and one of the Hilderbrand brothers said a week's salary. Bumchauls said if you do it I'll do it, because I am stronger than you are. I did not bet anyone. I wasn't too sure that I could lift it over my head. I knew that to do this everything had to work together and no errors.

I only made $1.15 per hour and I didn't have any money to bet with. I said well, I believe I will give it a try. We all came out of the little rec. room and it was only about 5 minutes before we started back to work. I walked over to the potato pile where the 100 pound bags of potatoes were. I looked up toward the boss' glass tower where he could see everything that was going on.

I realized then I had to do something and make the best of it, because the Big Boss was looking down at all of us not knowing what we all were up to. I came to the pile of 100 pound bags of potatoes and it was luck for me that a bag of potatoes was about waist high to shoulder high to me. I thought then that I had a chance. So I rolled the bag of potatoes close to me. I squatted down with my knees out a little and moved it over where I could get my palms under it. I had to be careful and I did not want those guys talking and laughing at me.

I got the bag sideways as close to me as I could and managed to get my hands just right where it was resting on my hands. With a quick jerk of my arms and up with my knees the bag of potatoes went over my head with my arms straight up and I held it there for a second or two. I let it down on the pile but it rolled lower than where it was when I lifted it.

Now they all started clapping their hands and then Bumchauis walked over to the pile with all the bags of potatoes. I knew that he could not manage to get that bag of potatoes up where he could lift it. He could not manage to lift it. The Big Boss walked over to me to shake my hand telling me he did not know how I did it. You might say that there was a trick to it. That was the talk around there for a long time.

Another Job:

I left the A & P a few months later and went to work with Sears Roebuck and Co. in the Automotive Department. This was at Cameron Village in Raleigh. I worked a few months with them at this store and I found out Sears was opening up a new store in Rocky Mount, NC.

I asked Mr. Hunter the store manager could I move to that location. He told me that he thought that I could be transferred to that store if Mr. Harris needed me. Mr. Hunter wrote Mr. Harris a letter about me. I took it to Mr. Harris and he read the letter and told me I had a job. He would need me in the Automotive and Tire Department Division 28 for automotive and department 95 for tires. It was two months before the store opened up so my job was setting up the Automotive Department and merchandising it with their assortment plans and layout according to the plan.

I worked with Sears almost nine years. I was a 5% commission salesperson and some weeks I made more than the department manager did, I was good at selling.

Moving on to Another Job:

I had a friend named Charles Peele that was working with the Montgomery Ward Company. He got in touch with me, he was a district manager for the catalogue department stores. I made an appointment to go to Baltimore to meet with the big boss Mr. Grady Burnes. He hired me on the spot. Montgomery Ward had a catalogue store in Little Washington, NC about 35 miles from Rocky Mount. I trained there under Doris Brooks to become a catalogue store manager. I commuted back and forth for about 4 weeks and by that time they had a location for me to manage.

After my training the company moved my family to Charlottesville, VA. We only lived there about 8 months. The manager in the Virginia Beach Catalogue Retail Store resigned and the company moved us again to the Virginia Beach area. I did not know that the Montgomery Ward Company was in such a mess with the management, shipping, merchandising, their credit department, and the whole company.

Montgomery Ward had over four hundred locations, retail and catalogue stores in the Eastern United States. We all worked out of the Baltimore Region, receiving merchandise for the stores and merchandise that customers order was the worst delivered services that I have ever seen.

More and more customers complained and there was no way to make them happy. While I was with Montgomery Ward many customers left them because of all their mix ups. I said to myself unless all this changes along with other problems Montgomery Ward will go out of business in years to come. This was in 1966 and 1967 that I was there. There was no way to get ahead with this company, so I resigned from Montgomery Ward.

I wrote J.C. Penny about a management position in one of their Auto Centers, being with Sears & Roebuck for nine years I did not see any reason why they would not hire me.

J.C. Penny was on this big expansion movement with opening up new stores and with detached auto centers with every retail store opening. This was good they became like Sears with adding hardware departments and auto centers to all the new locations. J.C. Penny at this time had this big expansion going on. Wouldn't it be something if the founder of J.C. Penny, Mr. James Cash Penny could come back now!!

Managements:

Having experience in automotive with Sears and in management with Montgomery Ward, I thought I could get a job with them. To be hired for a management position with J.C. Penny, they would make sure that you could handle it. I knew automotive and the procedures in running the center that I answered all the questions and added more about the business than what some of them knew.

They hired me for the Greenville, NC location. This was in Pitt Plaza Shopping Center on Greenville Blvd. This was a six bay detached auto store not too far from the street where cars could pull in right off the blvd for their gas and automotive needs. The big retail store was right behind me a short distance. All of the auto centers with J.C. Penny had gas. This was important to have gas it helped with the business.

I stayed with J.C. Penny for four years. Being 32 years old, I decided I could do better in business for myself. All during my early childhood I made my own money. So I decided to go in business for myself. I could not get it out of my bones. I wanted to be my own man.

I knew if I made anything out of myself and big money I had to practice what I knew in my own business.

The district manager of the auto center came by about every three months to discuss with me about sales management and whatever we need to talk about. We became close friends he was a little older than me. I was 32 and he might have been about 40. I thought he was a good honest person. He told me that the auto center was going to print a new TBA Manual (tires, batteries, and accessories) and bring it up to date and how the employees that worked in the auto center would get paid. This would be based on what their best position for them in automotive and procedures, how they could make more money.

This would include the sells people and also the mechanics. He said to his knowledge their salary will be based on suggested additional merchandise with this type of incentive program this would encourage every person to do a better job at selling. I told him that working with Sears almost 9 years I could add something to this new manual if he thought that it would be any good to do so.

He said that would not hurt to try. I told him that I would write up what I knew about working in the Sears Automotive Department. The two departments I worked in was (95 tires) and (28 auto accessories) as a 5% commissions salesman. Sears was big back in the 50' and 60's. I worked with them from 1957 until 1966. I told him that I would have it all written down and when he came again he could take it to the home office and see what they thought of it. He said that would be good. J.C Penny Auto Centers was something new to J.C Penny at that time.

In the early sixties J.C. Penny Co. was on this great expansion program opening up new Penny Stores everywhere and at each location they would have an auto center complete with gas. This would be just like Sears, except most of Sears Auto Centers did not have gas pumps.

I had a lot of procedures to write that consisted of inventory control, managements ordering merchandise, commission sales, and hourly pay incentives programs.

For example the sales people on the floor could get paid two different ways. They could get paid a regular salary plus 1% of their sales, most of the time this would be according to their experience. The salary would be about $60.00 per week.

On an average a sales person would sell about $1,500.00 worth of merchandise and at 1%, this would be $15.00 added to his $60.00 and that would give him $75.00 each week based on his sales. That was not too bad in the mid-sixties. The other salary for a sales person was 5%. But if he was a good sales person he could sell more than $1,500.00 worth of merchandise. You see their salaries are the same if their sales were the same $1,500.00 at 5% would equal $75.00. A commission sales person if he sold $2,000.00 worth he could make $100.00 a week salary.

Also we had more expensive items in the auto center and if you talked the customer up to a more expensive item this would be called a PM Item (Promotional Item) that will have a larger percent commission on it. I could write more about this.

Mechanic Pay:

We had incentives for the mechanic and they were good. When a vehicle came in the service center, we had what you called the Pitt Boss. The customer would come in mostly for one thing that he needed done or was wrong with his vehicle. We would take care and after that our mechanic would put the vehicles up on the rack and look good for bad mufflers, brake shoes, worn out or almost tail pipes, bad tires, grease job, oil change, an alignment to the front end or whatever it may be. They would be paid 1% on merchandise on whatever he found when he did the Pitt Boss. But labor to repair something or to install things like balancing a person's wheels and other things or just labor he would be paid 5%. A good mechanic usually made $80.00 per week but if he was good for one week, he could add $50.00 of PM to his salary and $130.00 a week would not be bad.

Everybody had to work together and be dedicated to his job and help each other. This helped make a good work place. We all made a little above average salaries in the auto center.

Back to my Good Friend:

I explained some of the things about running and managing an automotive center but there was a lot more to it. My friend came back in about three months and we got in my office and did a little heart to heart talking. I had everything written down, all my experiences with Sears and I added a little bit of my knowledge to it.

He said that this was good and the first chance he got he would take it to the home office. I told him that this might help me to manage a larger auto center with a J.C. Penny in a larger city. At that time they had auto centers that were twice bigger than the six bays I was managing in Greenville, NC. If they would move me to a 14 or 16 bay auto center I would stay with J.C Penny. I did not tell the district manager that I thought about leaving J.C. Penny.

After about three days with me he shook my hand and left. Well about 4 months latter J.C. Penny's new auto manual came out and about half of it was word for word what I had written up on several pages. Then it wasn't long after this my district manager got a new position in the home office because he re-wrote my procedures and signed his name to it. It was so good and well explained that they gave him this new position in the home office in Manhattan, New York. This is what your friends will do to you. I never heard from him again. I left 2 months later.

Back in the early days or up until about 1970, car engines didn't last long. If an engine got 50,000 miles before it started using oil, this was good. Back then the factories used this cast iron material and it would wear faster. The engine block where the pistons go up and down is what wears out. I can remember when you put a new engine in your car or bought a new car, you would have to drive the car slow for the first 500 miles until the rings seated to the pistons.

If or when it started using oil real bad, the engine block would need to be bored out and replaced with new sleeves to fit the bore and oversized pistons with chrome rings to fit the bore. This would last longer than the original engine that came with the car.

Most cars today have aluminum engines and they have a steel insert in the cylinders because it is more resistant to heat. If the steel inserts were not in the aluminum engine block the block would melt. Now you have a lighter engine and it will run cooler because of larger water ports going through the engine and better gas mileage and faster speed.

The last 50 years have come a long way with the making of engines.

The new developments in car engines today increases the power, durability, resistance to wear, and are more efficient to the engine. Today the cars' engines common alloy is aluminum which is lighter in weight.

The way engines are built today, the type of oil best to use is synthetic with better performance. It helps to protect the engine with less friction than the old non-detergent regular motor oil.

Cars today do not have the old type of carburetors. Whereas before many years ago the carburetors would put too much un-burnt fuel down in the cylinders walls for the spark plugs to ignite, wasting gas and at times engines would bleed out with too much gas. This would not give good mileage and would cause the engine cylinders to wear much quicker. This would be un-burnt fuel mixing with the oil and would cause the cylinder walls to wear much faster.

Today cars are made with fuel injectors that will burn all the fuel. With the injectors they would let just the right amount of fuel to the cylinder for the spark plug to ignite without wasting fuel. In the past, 50,000 miles was all an engine would do. Today they can go 500,000 miles with the electric and self driving car in today's world. With remote control and the help of satellite and navigational programs built in the cars, where will it all end? The GPS system is the best thing to travel with now and how the roads are built.

The self driving system on cars will need to detect the exact locations of the streets, intersections, and other cars approaching behind them. These directions are similar to the talking woman that tells you where to go, but this will not be telling humans what to do, it will be telling a machine and your life is in that machine's hands all the way!

I think sometimes it was better in the depression. I get the feeling that the way things are and all this tech knowledge, someday it will come crashing down on the whole wide world and this will be the end. As time goes on all these manmade tech things will become smarter than humans and there will be nothing we can do to stop it. It has been told that some of these things can repair themselves without man doing it. If you want to know the truth about how I feel, I am scared to death for this younger generation. (Is this good or bad? Time will tell.)

From my own opinion my prediction, the future wars will be fought with millions of drones throughout the world that will be so sophisticated that they will frighten our own imaginative intelligence. If we knew the truth right now the type of future direction that man has for us in the future, what would we do?

Man is getting too smart and dumb with it, that he will be unable to live in God's world because of his own destructive intelligence.

My First Business:

The First business was in the dry cleaning and Laundromat Business. I saw an ad where this dry cleaning company was looking for a manager or store owner. The company was out of Benson, NC. The name of the company was Banner Machinery. I called the owner Mr. Levenston and we talked about the business and he wanted me to come in the office and discuss this some more.

After meeting with him, he said that his company had several locations in Eastern NC. I didn't have any money to buy out one, but he liked me and offered me the store location in Rocky Mount, NC. He said the store had no manager, but the lady working there was doing a good job keeping it open. The store was costing him a lot of money because it was not paying its way. He said if someone would go in there and run the business and with some advertising, he believed the store could do a lot better.

He said the store had 7 people working there and if I got the store making money and paying all bills, that what was left I could have 50% for my pay. He said he did not want to close the business.

I accepted the offer and moved to Rocky Mount. It did not take me long to learn the business. I had 7 good ladies working there. The dry cleaning and Laundromat is a hard working business and it is a humid and a hot place to work.

It took lots of money to buy supplies, pay the employees, and electric bills. I knew that the business was off bad and it would take a lot of advertising to bring in the business. What I did, I advertised a 1 cent sale, this would be cleaning one item at regular price and charging 1 cent for a similar item. We were good to our customers and this ad brought in the business. It was all we could do to keep up with it. I only advertised the one cent sale once a month for three months. Each time and I began to see new faces all the time. The two for one sale did the job.

After about 4 months, I was paying the bills out of our bank account. We more than doubled the business. But there was one thing wrong I only had a small amount left over for my salary. Mr. Levenston was excited about what I had done because he did not have to take money from the company to pay for all their expenses at Rocky Mount location. This business did good for as long as I was there but I had to make a change.

I had a police officer friend that had his uniforms cleaned there and I asked him if I gave all the police officers a discount on their cleaning, could I get their business. He said he believed that I could, so he passed the word around to all the officers and they started coming into my location.

I gave them a 30% discount and we were doing good, bringing in more business. But after about one year, I was not making a good salary and I felt like that I gave this business all I had but I had to move on.

With three more Dry Cleaning and Laundromats in the area, I knew this was about all I could get. So it was not long that I found a buyer for the business. The buyer was a college professor at Weslayan College in Rocky Mount. He said he could teach college and run the business. So I stayed there another week teaching him everything I knew. It was good that all the employees liked him. He checked out my bookkeeping and expenses and he was happy the business was paying all the expenses. I do not know what happened after I left but I was gone to do better for myself.

Rack Display Business:

In the year 1970, I started another business. This was called a Wholesale Rack Jobbing Business, displaying ladies hosiery and men's socks on a swivel display rack. This way a person could turn the rack around and this would help sell the merchandise better. They could see the different socks, hosiery, and the color all on one display. I set them up in the heavy traffic areas.

People did not have buying ladies hosiery and socks on their minds when they went into the store, but seeing the display they changed their minds and some would buy. This is what you would call impulse buying. I would service the stores about every two to three weeks.

I put displays in Mom and Pop Stores, convenient stores, super markets, truck stops, and drug stores. I traveled all parts of Eastern NC from Raleigh to the coast. I purchased my merchandise from the Burlington area from two hosiery mills, Freeman and Bennett Hosiery Mills. I stayed with this business for thirteen years. I bought a house in the doctors' and lawyers' area. I wanted to make a change so I decided to get my real estate license, where I thought the big money was.

This is when President Regan was President and interest rates went up to 18% on house loans. I found out quick that this is not where the big money was. Most people were not buying or selling their houses because of the interest rates.

Making a Change With My Life:

In the year 1980, my wife and I separated. I moved down to the Emerald Isle Beach away from Rocky Mount, NC to our place at the beach. I continued on with my route business and left the big house in the doctors' and lawyers' area to her.

After about two more years in my business I decided to sell my hosiery business. I found a buyer in the Wilson, NC area and after seeing and understanding the business, he bought the business.

His name was Floyd and he had retired from Pepsi Cola Company early and he was about 60 years old. He said after being on the road with Pepsi Cola, this would be a business he would like.

After 13 years, I began to have second thoughts about selling it because it was a good business. I wanted to make a change, so I did. Two years before I sold my business I got my Commercial Fishing License. I knew this would be something I could fall back on if and when I did sell my hosiery business.

The boat that I had would do fine catching clams, shrimp, and scallops. I was selling my catch to the local fish market in the Cape Carteret area and I did good doing this. After about two years, I met a friend by the name of Pat Finn on the water. He asked me did I know that some of the guys had gone to Florida to clam. I told him I had not seen Peter Mann lately and he said that he was one of them and they were in the Melburne, Florida area. He said that he was going down there the following week.

I found out where Peter was living in Florida. It was a small community by the name of Grant, Florida. I gave him a call and he told me to come on down and bring a good clamming boat, that they were doing good It wasn't long before I got everything ready and I closed up my place here on Emerald Isle and I told my neighbor to look after my place and send me my mail.

I got down there in the month of June 1984. After rigging up my boat for clamming and obtaining my Florida Commercial Fishing License from the Fishery Department, I began digging for clams all through the rest of the summer. I did good until the first winter. I was there the winter of 1984 and 1985. It was one of the coldest winters on record that Florida ever had.

I didn't do much clamming in the winter months but I still made a little money with a few good weather days. It began to warm up fast in the spring of 1985. During this year Florida had over 5,000 clammers on the Indian River catching clams. Indian River was a big river from about 2 miles wide in some places. In December it got so cold ice was freezing right on into January of 1986. It was freezing on the roads and inside my boat.

I was living in the Bearfoot Bay Subdivision, a big mobile home subdivision. Behind my doublewide mobile home I had 2 orange trees about 6 to 8 feet high. It got so cold that the orange trees had ice sickles 5 to 6 feet long hanging from them all the way to the ground, touching the ground and about as round as a soft ball. The limbs were bent downward almost breaking from the tree.

Trees that were native to Florida that had been there over a hundred years froze and died. Once again this winter was so cold we did not do much clamming. If I was not on the Indian River clamming, I was in the pool room shooting pool. Bearfoot Bay had this nice recreation center and it was nice. It was hard to catch clams being this cold. They would go down in the mud bottom of the river too far for the clam rake teeth to reach them.

I can remember this dude that thought he was good shooting pool. So I played him. We matched to see who was going to shoot first. This game was who got the most points won the game. I broke the rack of balls and made two on the break. I ran the table putting every ball in the pockets and I won the pot, but it was only a dollar. He said he had never seen anybody that could that, so he would not play me anymore. He did not know that this was only a few times in my life that I did this.

Space Challenger Disaster:

Several days during the summer of 1985, out on Indian River I witnessed the space ships go up from the launch pad at Cape Canaveral Kennedy Space Center. I got so use to it sometimes I did not even watch them into space.

On this particular cold morning of January 28, 1986, it was cold with ice everywhere. I bundled up good and decided to go clamming because it had been several days since I had been. If the clams were not up a little I would take my boat out and come back to Barefoot Bay. At the boat ramp there was a big open space right off US One Highway where lots of trucks and cars could park. It was a little late when I got there hoping it would warm up some so I could go clamming. There were a lot of cars and people there. I realized that this morning they were going to shoot the space ship up. I remember they had washed it down two or three times to go up, but at the last minute they changed their mind, but this time was the real thing.

They all were standing outside of their cars to watch for it. The time now was 11:38 when they launched it. This is what I saw. By watching the others this one was a little different. It was a little lower and had a much longer and brighter tail of fire flying it and to me it seemed a little bit slower going up into space.

People got excited when they saw it coming from the horizon. It looked like it was right over our heads, but it was out over the ocean about 12 miles from where we were standing. Seventy-three seconds into the flight it blew up, I saw a big huge cloud of smoke. Right at this instance I could not see the space ship, but quickly I saw pieces of things falling from the smoke cloud. The two rockets that propel it were going up their separate ways one a far distance from the other once they got out of the burst of clouds that it made when it exploded. I turned around and the gentlemen that were next to me, I told him that the space ship blew up. He asked me "how did I know?" I said that I had seen them go up before and this was different. I told him to turn his car radio on and I hollowed at everybody to turn their radios on that the space ship had blown up.

People standing around did not know what had happened and sure enough they were announcing on the radio that the space ship exploded soon after launch. I noticed a lot of people began to cry and you could tell that from the space watchers this would be a sad day in history. I left and went back to my house and all the neighbors around me were talking about it. They could not believe that I witnessed it beside Indian River.

My Second Wife:

I met my wife to be in November 1984, a few months after moving down to Florida. We saw each other occasionally and as time went on we became a little closer, but not serious. It took another year before we realized that we liked each other a great deal.

In September of 1986, we moved back to the Raleigh, NC area. I got a job with Parrish Realtor, now again this is when Regan was President and the interest rate was still around 18% on house loans. I only stayed in the Real Estate business with Parrish Realtor about one year. I knew that I had to do something else.

They did not want me to leave. I was good in Real Estate, but not good enough to suit me. Out of 12 realtors, after a year I was third in listing and sales. I even had a fellow realtor that named me his "HERO". He said he wanted to be just like me in Real Estate. He did not want me to leave. I told him that I appreciated his kindness but that Real Estate was just too slow for me, I had to move on.

Another Business:

I observed while being in Real Estate that it was difficult to find good people to clean and do repair on vacant homes. At this time we bought a house in the old farm acre area north of Smithfield about 28 miles from Raleigh. Sue and I started a new business and we named it the Smithfield Janitorial Service.

I told Parrish Realtors that I wanted their business and we did jobs for them and other Real Estate Companies. We had jobs from the Smithfield, Clayton, and on into the Raleigh area. The word got out that we did a good job. I had some circulars printed up, mailed them, hand delivered them to a lot of places, hung them on doors, and gave them to the business owners also.

It wasn't too long before Quail Properties on the Old Wake Forest Road wanted us to do some of their cleaning and repair work. Within a few weeks, they were giving us more than Sue and I could do. We had to hire a man to help me and a young lady to help Sue.

Quail Properties was a big Rental Company and when people moved out they wanted us in there immediately to clean, clean the carpet, and to do minor repairs so it would not stay vacant long. When I met Sue, my wife, in Florida she was in the cleaning business there. We both made a perfect team.

We worked the business for about five years. We decided we wanted to move to the Emerald Isle area. That is where I moved from when I went to Florida. It did not take long to sell my business because it was a ready-made business. When we moved to Emerald Isle area we started another cleaning business in the Cape Carteret area and on the beach. This went on for about two years and I sold that business because we saw a better opportunity. Boy didn't this one pay off for us.

Flea Market Business:

At this time the Flea Market Business was a big business. This was about 1993. We rented a big space in this huge building in Jacksonville, NC about 20 miles from where we lived. We obtained a wholesale booklet that had things that we could sale. The Flea Market business took off good. We picked out a few good things that sold. In the Flea Market Business it is not how many items you have to sell it's the merchandise that is selling. So we concentrated on our best sellers, pushed them hard, and ran specials all the time.

Being in the Rack Jobbing Business in the past I saw something that caught my eye. I ordered a display rack and 180 Foil Print Pictures from Dolan Sports out of New Jersey. I displayed them on the swivel type racks, it held 90 pictures. Boy did they sell like hot cakes. We purchased all types. They had Ethnic Pictures, some of Martin Luther King. These pictures were hand etched by hand on aluminum foil. They were called foil print pictures.

They were selling so good I asked myself, could I take them on the road and start another wholesale route business. I decided to do this. I contacted some of my old customers that I had sold to in the past. They said they would give it a try and see how they would sale. This gave me a start to establish this Picture Route Business.

In order to accomplish this I needed a big van with lots of space. I purchased a good used step van that would carry my displays and had enough room for my pictures. With these head high 36 pocket racks they would hold three pictures in each pocket and it would swivel around that made it easy for the customers to find the one they wanted. Within six months on the road, I told Sue that we will close up the Flea Market and she had to help me. The Foil Print Pictures were still selling good at the Flea Market. This told me that they should sell good throughout my route.

After closing up the Flea Market, Sue became my Warehouse Manager because when we received a shipment someone had to be there. I purchased my pictures from Dolan Sports out of New Jersey. At times Sue would ride with me if we had no shipment on the way. I had my displays in heavy traffic areas in the big box stores, Wal-Mart, truck stops, and large super markets from my Raleigh and Goldsboro Routes.

I decided to stop at the Wal-Mart store in Jacksonville this was my first Wal-Mart Store. I didn't think they would buy from me because I was not a big company. The store manager was a nice small black manager. This was about 3:00 pm on a Friday. After introducing myself, I asked him would he look at my pictures. He said he was busy but I told him I had some samples in a little kasha case that it would only take a minute to see them. He looked at all of them along with the Martin Luther King pictures and this was a beautiful picture of Martin Luther King. He liked this picture. I told him and showed him display racks I had in other locations. He asked if they did not sell would I pick them up. I told him if they did not sell I would pick them up and he would not owe me a cent of what did sell off the rack.

I told him I would put a display in on consignment and if they did not sell in a week I would pick them up. He said that he would try a rack of them. And then he asked if they sold good how often could I come by because the company did not want empty shelves and racks. I told him being this closed to him that I could check on the pictures every week.

He agreed to that if they sold good he would like to have them in the store. I know that this was the first step to a big opportunity with Wal-Mart if they did good in this store because this District Manager had along with the Jacksonville store about eight other Wal-Mart stores in a wide area.

He asked me what would be his mark-up percent. I asked him what would be fair with Wal-Mart. He said that he would like to sell them cheaper than my other locations and I agreed to that. I sold them at other places for retail $6.99 and $7.99. He said lets go with $5.97 and if I could give him a 37% mark-up, this was good. We both agreed to that. He told me to set it up in the front part of the store near the cash registers.

The following week when I came off my route and went by the Wal-Mart Store in Jacksonville every picture on the rack was gone. He asked me if I could fill that display up and put another one in beside it. This was good. The store manger could buy things local like plants and flowers. He told me to meet him in his office and he would pay me for the first display and also these two displays. He paid me out of his local garden money that he had in his petty cash. All total he paid me $1,940.00 and from that time on the District

Manager had me to put displays in all his 9 Wal-Mart locations that he managed.

The District Manager told the Home office how good they were selling and within a month I had pictures in all the locations that I could hand service on my route. I traveled parts of SC, NC, and VA. I had to be out of town for 2 to 3 nights a week. I had to put extra heavy duty springs on my step van.

With two to three thousand pictures and with a glass and metal frames they were heavy. I serviced the Wal-Mart Stores and other accounts for almost 7 years. The last year I worked my route I bought out a 10 acre Mobile Home Park because my Mobile Home Park needed me more and more it was too much for me to do both. I saw where I could expand the park and put more homes in there. It wasn't long before I sold the business (Foil Print Picture Business) to a local fellow with Wal-Mart's approval to keep the pictures in the stores.

George who bought my pictures worked the Wal-Mart Stores and the other accounts for about five more years. He sold the business to someone else and then he went in business with his brother in the Plumbing Business. We both did good with that Picture Route Business.

From time to time I saw the pictures in the Wal-Mart Stores for about three or four years in this location. Then it got where I could not see them in the stores anymore. I don't know what happened to that business.

Owning a Mobile Home Park:

I purchased the Mobile Home Park in 1994. The park had only 9 mobile homes in it. The park was in bad condition. The old man Mr. Neff that owned the park did not keep it clean and neat. The park had about 7 acres cleared and three in the woods at the back of the park that could be used to expand.

I moved three of the 9 homes out and the "trash" people with them. My park was only three miles from the beach of Emerald Isle, NC in the Cape Carteret area. I worked with this 7 acre area to move more mobile homes in there.

It took me about three years to put all the homes I could on the seven acres. It was tough getting approval from the Environmental Health Department to install septic tanks and run 2 each 60 feet septic lines to each home. This was slow going. I did all the electric hookups, plumbing, water lines, and under pinning myself. Everything had to be inspected by the Electric Company and Environmental Health Department. I purchased good used 2 bedroom homes for my park. With two bedrooms homes I could put two on each septic system. A single wide mobile home just is not big enough for three bedroom homes. This way you would have more room for the living room, kitchen, and bedrooms if they had 2 baths.

At the end of five years, I had all the homes paid for and I was making good money. The income helped me to purchase two farms. For about 9 years I owned the Mobile Home Park.

I purchased a farm in Halifax County and one in Terrill County. I leased them out and made a good income from that. Both farms had bears, deer, ducks, and just about any animal that you would find in the State of NC. My son, grandson, and I had good places to hunt. We had a camper on the farms.

We all three bagged some pretty trophy bucks. After five years I sold one of the farms and kept the other one another five years. This one I sold to hunters and it had geese, ducks, and bears. It joined thousands of acres of land that belonged to the state and by my farm joining the state land I could hunt that too.

I got lost one night in the woods for four hours and when the wind stopped blowing I could hear things far away. I was a little scared, I was by myself. After hearing the sound of things about 9 or 10 o'clock that night I figured out how to come out of the woods. I was about one mile from the camper and ½ mile in the woods.

Duck Impoundment:

After I purchased the farm I found out that it could be qualified for a Duck Impoundment. Back then the Government would pay to dig out and fix the high sides with a big farrow of dirt all around it The dirt would come out of the enclosed area with a deep ditch about 10' deep and 20' wide. It was deep enough for water to come from the ground and fill it up throughout with about 2' of water in it all times.

The reason for this was to bring back some of our wild habitats for ducks and wild animals. Wild grass and marsh type grass will grow inside it and also planted wild rice. At one corner of the Impoundment they installed a water gate below the bottom of the Impoundment to let the water out in the spring then you can plant milo, millet, corn, wheat, and other grains.

When all the grains began to fill out in the fall you placed the boards back at the corner of the Impoundment. You may also plant different types of grains on the high levels around the Impoundment. The food will bring in ducks of all kinds to feed in the Impoundment. In the deep ditch around the Impoundment will make a good fishing place for bass, brims, and catfish.

The size of the Impoundment was 10 acres. After about 6 years I sold this farm to a family who loved to duck hunt more than eat when they are hungry. I went back about five years later. At the time I built the Duck Impoundment the Government also planted 30 acres of Pine seedlings. This cost a lot but you had to sign an agreement that you will keep it this way for 20 years. I think if you kept it that long you would continue on keeping it without destroying this Habitat.

The people I sold the farm to had a beautiful Habitat for animals; ducks, deer, bears, minks, otters, muskrats, weasels, foxes, coyotes, coons, wild turkeys, and a lot of other animals. This farm was down 94 Highway near Mattamuskeet Lake where it has always been a fly over for wild geese and ducks to come or migrate from Canada in the winter and migrate back for the summer. The Duck Impoundment was only a few miles from Mattamuskeet Lake and the fly over from the lake to feed around my Duck Impoundment and former fields were astronomical I sold the farm for big bucks.

I had my Mobile Home Park for almost 9 years and I kept it clean. My Mobile Homes were spaced apart from each other and this was good. I had grass growing throughout the years and I had lots of trees for shade. People began to notice my park and I had no problem renting the homes. One day I got a phone call out of the blue from a fellow asking me if I would consider selling my park. He told me that he had come into a little money and he wanted to invest in something near the beach. I told him that I would think about it but I had not thought about selling it. He said if I decide to sell it let him know before he invested in something else.

This was on a Friday and Sue and I had plans to go to Hawaii on the following Monday and stay a week. We flew to Hawaii and he called me on that Thursday about my park. I told him that I would let him know something the following week. I told Sue that he wanted it bad. Sue agreed that if I could sell it for a good price let it go. Most of the time when you bought a home or sold one you could get a comparable price similar to yours to help make up your mind, but a Mobile Home Park, I had no comparison.

I had in mind the price I thought I wanted for the Mobile Home Park, but I knew that things were changing fast down near the beach and real estate was beginning to be really good down here. I did a lot of thinking should I sell it or should I keep it. Sue said that I had a good buyer in hand now and if and when I might want to sell the park later, I might not find a good buyer.

I broke things down in the park, what was the 10 acres worth, what were the 17 Mobile Homes worth, and most of all what was the rental income that I was getting from the Mobile Homes would be worth. This was a good income month after month and it will always be there.

The price I had in mind, I did not think that this was enough. So if I priced it too high I could come down a little but if I priced it too low I could not go up and I would be sorry. The price I had in mind I thought was a fair price. So I decided to add $100,000.00 to it. Sue and I talked about that and she did not think that I could get over a half million dollars for it but it would not hurt to try. I called him and told him that I had a price, for him to come over, and we would talk about things.

I told him the price I would sell it to him for and he thought a minute, running everything in his mind such as the taxes, income, and other things. He agreed to buy it for that price. After closing and a few weeks later, I wondered if I had sold it too cheap.

We moved to New Bern, NC after selling the park in the year October 2002. My wife had been working or employed with Moen Faucet Company for about 10 years. We moved to the New Bern area out in the country near Moen Faucet Company. This was good because it only took her 10 minutes to get to work while living down at the beach area it took her 35 minutes. We bought a big house with about 19,000 square feet and it was on 2 acres of land with upstairs and a big swimming pool.

I was in my late sixties and now I had nothing to do. I had taught myself how to weld when we had the park I decided that I would make Bar-B-Que grills. I needed 55 gallon oil drums for patio grills and 250 gallon drums for pig cookers. I went around to oil companies and bought up a few drums.

I bought all my supplies from Springs Axils Wheels and Welding Rods. I started building the patio grills and pig cookers. Along with building the cookers, I built a lot of picnic tables. I did all this for about 4 years. I decided that I was almost working for nothing because the supplies and boards for the tables were costing more than what I could sell my cookers and tables for and come out with a reasonable profit, so I ended this job.

It was not long before I became bored and I decided to look for a job in Real Estate this would be easy work for me. I was not an in-house person I had to find me a job. This time I would not be self-employed but this would be okay. At least this would get me out of the house.

I was looking at the New Bern paper and I stumbled across this maintenance job with a Real Estate Company that needed help with the rental units.

I was getting old, but in good health. I decided to call the owner of the business. She answered the phone and I asked her about the job. She asked me what I could do. I told her just about anything that she wanted me to do. I told her that I had been an Entrepreneur most all my life and had done maintenance work off and on for many years.

She told me to come in and talk to her that she thought we could get together. I said to her if she had a limit on how old a person needed to be, that I was 72. She said that wasn't too old and I did not sound like I was 72.

The next day I went into talk to her and she came out of her office and looked at me and asked me to come in her office. All she asked me was what I thought how much money I should be paid.

I knew about what maintenance workers pay was in the New Bern area. I had some friends that said if you made $13.00 per hour it was good. This was the year 2008. I told her I thought that I should get between $12.00 to $13.00 dollars per hour, she said that was good. She would split the difference and pay me $12.50 per hour, I accepted.

I worked with her doing maintenance and inspecting rental homes for wear and tear. I also helped the other maintenance people do things they didn't know. I worked with her for four years and by then my knees began to bother me. I loved the job but I knew I had to resign from the job.

I told her the problems and she understood and told me that I was the best and a tough person. She said that if I decided that I wanted my job back to come on in and sign in and go to work that I did not have to talk to her. This was a good feeling to hear this from her.

My wife had worked for Moen Faucet Company for almost 20 years by now. "Man how time goes by." I got old and did not realize I was getting old. Now I was 76 and we moved back to the beach in a beautiful gated subdivision. Sue retired form Moen Faucet Company about a year later. She worked to the age that was required for her so she could receive all her Social Security. We had a lot of friends here because of living here a few years ago, Sue and I made lots of friends.

My Last Business:

A few months after moving back to the beach area, it did not take long before I became bored again. I started looking for something my wife and I could do together. We were in Jacksonville, NC at the Lowes Building Material and this older gentleman by the name of Marvin was selling hot dogs.

This caught my attention and my wife and I walked up to the hot dog cart and both of us observed everything. We checked out the cart, how he waited on customers, and in general the whole set up the way he was doing things. We bought a hot dog each from him and it didn't take long to make friends with him being about the same age he was.

He told me that there was another Lowes on the other side of town and there was not one set up there to sale hot dogs. I told him that I might decide to get in the business. The next day I went to the Health Department to see what type of permits and license I needed.

The lady I talked to was really nice and she said that the next thing I needed to do was to buy a hot dog cart. But before I could put it anyplace that they would have to look at it and approve it because it had to be constructed the right way in order for them to approve it.

I went on line and found a good used one in the Raleigh area. It was almost new. I called the phone number and asked the gentleman would he take pictures of it and send the pictures to my phone he said he would. After receiving the pictures I went back to the Health Department and they looked at them and they were impressed with them. They told me that they would approve this hot dog cart. I will tell you now the Health Department will have everything 100% the right way or no way at all.

I called this gentleman back and told him that I would buy the cart and to meet me in Smithfield, NC, and I would pay him cash. I took the cart to Jacksonville, NC and they approved the cart. I got all my permits and license for the county.

My intention was to put my hot dog cart at the other Lowes location but before all this was completed and all the paperwork was approved, I started thinking about Camp Lejeune Marine Corps Base near Jacksonville, NC., I asked my son what did he think about me getting on the base with my hot dog cart. He told me it might be hard to do because I had not been in any type of service.

My son Brian had 13 years in the CB, this was (Construction Battalion), and he told me if I could put my hot dog cart on the base that I would do good. I went for it. I called the Health Department Food Supply Office on the base and talked to Mr. Rogers.

He said his assistant was on vacation and she would be the one to talk to. He would leave her a message to call me when she came back. She called me the following week and told me to bring my hot dog cart on the base so they could look at it. She told me what building to go to and when I got to the entrance have them to call her because that was the only way that I could get on the base without a base pass and I.D.

I got on base and I went to the building she told me to go to. She met me out there along with one of the Health Department Officials. They passed my hot dog cart. She said that this was only the first step because my wife and I had to take a food course and we had to pass with at least an 80 score out of 100. She said this would be a three day course and there would be about 15 to 20 people taking the course.

I agreed to that and we both passed the Health Food Class with high scores. This course dealt with just about everything that you could imagine. After the course she told me where to put the hot dog cart. About 12 months ago there was one near the Commissary and he did good.

After the first week they came by to check it out. They were impressed with how everything looked. They checked out the coolers, all the food temperatures of everything, checked all the condiments, and the safety of the hot dog cart. They gave me an A plus rating certificate to go on the cart where it could be seen. They told me that they would check out the cart from time to time without me knowing when they would come.

We purchased all our supplies from the Sam's Club Wal-Mart. We kept the cart on the Camp Lejeune Corps Base for two years. We made good with all the sport games and events. The biggest one day take was fourteen hundred and sixty-five dollars, not bad for two dollar dogs, and one dollar drinks, chips, and water. We had to resign the next summer because it got so hot I almost passed out. The doctor advised me to do so.

Figure 49 Author at 21 years of age

Figure 50 Left to right - The author, sister
Laura, brother Roy and brother LB

Figure 51 Left to right - Author at six, LB, Laura, Roy, and dog Joe

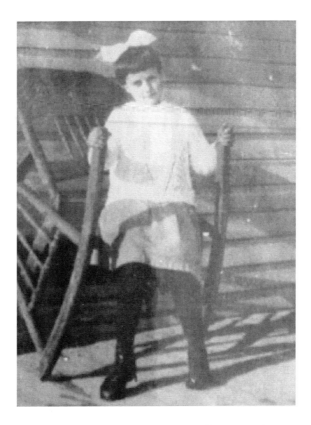

Figure 52 Nancy Carter Woodard, my mother at twelve years old

Figure 53 Author's Mother and Father

Figure 55 Author and his lovely wife Sue

Figure 56 Merlon and wife Sue

Figure 57 The Author's wife Sue

Figure 58 Brother LB and the Author

Figure 59 My children from left to right - Reggie at 16 years old, Tammy at 8 years old, and Brian at 12 years old.

Figure 60 Author claiming on Indian River in Florida

Figure 61 A boat load of clams

Figure 62 Clam boats going out to clam from the boat dock on the Indian River

Figure 63 Clams harvested in Indian River, FL

Figure 64 Standing in water clamming with a 22" Bull rake

Figure 65 Family pig picking – so good!

Figure 66 A grill the author made

Figure 67 Another grill made by the Author

Figure 68 A utility trailer the Author built

Figure 69 Seventeen years later still looks good

My Ancestry DNA
Part Two

By

Merlon Patrick Woodard

My Ancestry DNA:

A larger percentage of Mom's DNA comes from Northwestern Europe, England, and Wales.

Fifteen to twenty thousand years ago human migration was taking place throughout the world. The History of Britain began over 12,000 years ago when the Glacial Ice was recorded and the sea levels went down low enough for the Stone Age hunters-gatherers to cross from Mainland Europe to Britain on foot.

At this time in history people had no domesticated animals to make it easier for them to travel. Most of the time when migration existed throughout the world, different tribes of people came across other tribes of people that were already there. This is when war would break out with the invaders until one side got the upper hand on the other and this would change people's way of life. Many humans died because of human migration from one part of the world to another part of the world. Eventually over a period of time they learned to live together. Different tribes of people are what made up the history of Britain, the heart of our England and Wales region. As groups of invaders invaded the native population, some of the Invaders were the Romans, Anglo Saxons, Vikings, and the Nomans. They left this mark on Britain both politically and culturally. History tells us that the earliest population weren't wiped out but adopted to the New World with the new arrivals.

My Ancestry DNA:

A smaller percentage of Mom's DNA came from Ireland and Scotland

After the Ice Age Glaciers retreated from Northern Europe more that 9,000 years ago, hunter-gathers spread north into part of Great Britain, Ireland, and Scotland. This is similar to the migration that occurred with Northwestern Europe, England, and Wales which they all make up the United Kingdom.

During the Middle Stone Age, some 3,000 years later and during the New Stone Age, the first farming communities appeared in Ireland. The Bronze Age began 4,500 years ago and brought with it new skills, linked to metal working and pottery. During the late Bronze Age, iron was discovered in mainland Europe and a new cultural phenomenon began to evolve.

As more humans left the early stages of their life thousands of years earlier, they became more intelligent and civilized. They began to settle down from a type of nomadic life style, learned how to make things, and farmed their land with cows, sheep, and other animals. They also became herders. This is when colonization came about.

Being able to trade with other people in other regions was one of the biggest improvements human made for their futures years of survival and existence.

Ethnic Ancestry (Mom's People):

A small percentage of Mom's DNA came from the Benin and Togo people of the Ivory Coast of East Africa.

Benin sits just west of Nigeria and west of Benin is Togo. Benin has a population of 9.88 million at this time that is growing at an annual rate of 2.84%. Togo is only slightly behind with a growth rate of 2.73% and has 7.15 million people. Both of the little countries or regions are largely rural areas but more densely concentrated along the coast.

Though tied closely together by history, geography, and religion, the inhabitants of Benin and Togo are ethnically quite different. Distant trading partners have long been part of Africa's fabric this is especially true of West Africa's fabric. When migration conquests and intermarriage within Allied Kingdoms helped explain why for example 43% of people from our Benin/Togo region have DNA that looks similar to the profile for our Ivory Coast Ghana region and 20% appears to have links to our profile for Nigeria.

Benin/Togo Region near the East Coast of Africa lived on the edge of thick forest where the resources were rich and they could supplement their diets with bush meat, ape, chimpanzees, gorillas, monkeys, antelopes, buffalo (water), elephants, birds, crocodiles, tortoises and wild pigs.

These tribal people go back over 30,000 years ago with hundreds of different tribes throughout this great Africa Continent. The different tribes did not know who their enemies were. First, like all other parts of the world and even in the USA back thousands of years ago, right on up to when Columbus discovered America there were many different tribes of Indians in America. They fought among themselves killing each other, taking hostages from other tribes, and even the women they took became wives to some of the Indian men folk.

It was the African tribes to kill first and capture as many of the other tribe members as they could. This is the way it was, that they did not know any better.

Cannibalism was practiced in most all Africa in the past and other parts of the world. Cannibalism is still going on today in some parts of Africa and throughout the world.

In the jungles of Papua New Guinea at of the turn of the 20st Century different tribes tried to kill and capture as many as they can of the other tribes. This is what happened to Nelson Rockefeller's son off the coast of New Guinea. "This story will be later on in this book."

Ethnic Ancestry (Mom's People)

Another small percentage of Mom's DNA comes from the Cameroon Congo and the Southern Bantu people.

Their location centered near the Ivory East Coast of Africa and extended into the Central parts of Africa with their region joining the Benin-Togo region. With these little countries in close proximity of each other the African people intermarried and so on for thousands of years that lived within adjoining regions of each other.

For 30,000 years or more this Africa Cameroon Congo Basin has been the home for these African people before the Great Migration over 3,000 years ago. There were over 250 tribes or ethnic groups with more than 500 languages and more than 300 million people speak Bantu languages.

The Eastern Bantu people learned how to grow grain as they migrated east toward the Great Lakes region in modern day Uganda, Kenya, and Jangonia. There they learned how to smelt iron and make a kind of steel. Reliable tools combined with farming and herding skills led to a growing population which kept the Bantu Groups moving south from the Cameroon Basin and some migrated back west toward the Atlantic Ocean.

The Bantu and the Benin/Togo African people were more civilized than the Bushmen Tribes throughout Africa because of more foreigners. They had more exposure to the British, Arabs, and Portuguese merchants as trading partners.

Michael Rockefeller:

Michael was the son of Nelson Rockefeller born May 18, 1938, presumed to have died on November 19, 1961. He was the fifth child of the New York Governor and future US Vice President.

He disappeared during an expedition in the Asmat region of Southwestern Netherlands, New Guinea, which is now a part of the Indonesian Province of Papua. His mission was to collect artifacts from visiting different Asmat Villages.

Michael was accompanied by his Dutch friend Rene' Wassing a Dutch government anthropologist.

This is how Michael died at the hands of the Asmat Tribesmen people in New Guinea. Michael's wooden Catamaran boat was overturned by a storm off the Coast of New Guinea. He was exploring the region for some primitive art work for the new museum that had recently opened in New York. He told his friend Rene' Wassing that he would take two empty gas cans and swim ashore for help. His friend advised him not to do it because some boat will see us and rescue us.

Michael decided to go ahead and using the gas cans swam several miles to shore. The Asmat Tribesmen were on their canoes near the shore when they saw Michael close to shore.

With fear and excitement they had never seen a white man before. These Aboriginal New Guinea Natives used their dugout canoes to navigate off shore a distance to spear turtles, sharks, and certain types of fish. The dugout canoes were long and carved out in the center with an iron axe. It required a tall tree mostly a Sycamore Tree for the best canoes. They were hard and strong wood and would not rot or soak with water. They would work fine with as many as 20 natives riding in them depending on how tall the tree was. The New Guinea Savages would use these canoes to supply their needs for food and war.

These Cannibalism New Guinea Savages would kill and eat other tribe members in the jungles and take their women folk into their tribes, rape them and use the hair, bones, and skull for ornaments.

They speared Michael and took him ashore to the tribal leader. All the tribe natives danced around with excitement with what they were doing to Michael. Michael tried to swim for his life after realizing that the Savages were out to spear him. He was speared through his ribs, his head was scalped, he was cut across his face from his nose to the nape of his neck, and cooked along with other parts of his body.

His ribs were cut out with an axe, his arms and legs were cut off, and his entrails pulled out while all the men were shouting and dancing. The tribesmen savagely used Michael's blood and covered parts of their bodies with it. After they cooked Michael's body, the Tribal Leader ate his brains. They all feasted on his meat. They used his bones and skull for ornaments.

The practice of Cannibalism exists today in New Guinea and other parts of the world. Here are eight hot spots where cannibals dine on people among their friends. The first is Papuea New Guinea, Flgi Island, the Ganges River of India, the Democratic Republic of the Congo, Cambodi, Nuku Hiva, French Polynesia, Siberia, and Rotenburg Germany. This is just a little part of what humans can do to humans.

Humans will never become civilized as long as humans stay on the face of the Earth. A dog can be taught to do things better than humans.

East Coast of Africa:

This is where Mom's people's ancestries came away on slave ships in the late 1600's and early 1700's.

The first slaves were brought to America by a Dutch boat in 1619 to the British Colony of Jamestown, Virginia. The slave boat left 20 slaves in the British Colony.

This was a New World. This would be the place to bring slaves to.

After this the year 1619, the slave trade went on for over 300 years throughout North, Central, and South America. There were ships from countries all over the world, ships from Britain, Portuguese, Dutch, and other parts of the world transporting African people to many countries.

(This is a thought) With ships picking up slaves from Coastal regions why did it take Columbus to discover America in the year 1492 this long?

To trade for goods was what the slave trade was all about. There was not any type of money back then. It was precious metals, gold, silver, and food. They traded for sugar, salt, tobacco, coal, Rum, molasses, and hard liquor. The liquor would get the African people drunk and this would make it easier to take them aboard their ships. They also brought from Africa; rice, okra, black eye peas, yams, kidney beans, and lima beans, to try planting in the new world. They also brought peanuts, millet, watermelon, and other seeds.

Captured:

The African people did not have many ways of defending themselves during slavery times. Each tribe stood alone more or less like wild animals. They had this culture that had been handed down from generation to generation.

Some ways African people became slaves, they would be captured in war between different tribes. The tribal leader would sell them to slave ships for mostly hard liquor. This is a way they sold the slaves and less of the slaves would not get killed in their little wars between the tribes. The slave would be traded for alcohol, ornaments, and different types of food and clothing from the New World.

Many times the children would be left behind if they were not at least 8 years old. The slave trade went on throughout the world not only in the New World but the slave business went on a thousand years before the New World existed.

All countries needed people for hard labor work. The African people were well suited for this type of labor because surviving in the jungles they became strong with lots of muscle power. Sometimes being a slave was better than living in the jungles and trying to defend yourself from other tribes. If it were not for the mulo and slavery it would have taken hundreds of more years for our nation to be as great as it is today.

The journey between Africa and the New World could take 8 to 10 weeks on sailing ships or longer depending on the ocean weather. Ocean storms were the biggest problem crossing the ocean.

The slaves were chained together and crowded closely with no room to move. They would set and lay in their own filthy condition.

Many starved to death and they had to be thrown overboard along with the weak ones. Thousands died in theses harsh conditions. They were treated less than animals and for many years slaves were considered animals not human.

All African Americans were not slaves. They were more not slaves than the ones that were slaves. Most plantation owners made them into slaves living under their rules and the African people had no choice.

More African people worked for landowners growing crops, raising and herding animals, working in sugar cane fields, and lots of other things such as building roads.

The North had more African Americans during slavery time than the South. There were more shipping ports in the North than in the South. The ports were New York, Philadelphia, Baltimore, and Boston. In the South were Charleston, SC and New Orleans.

Not only did slaves work on plantations some worked in coal mines. Lots of non-slaves worked in gold mines, coal mines, sugar cane fields, and turpentine forests. Tar was made from turpentine extracted from pine trees.

Turpentine was also made into solvents, fuel, and cooked into tar. This required many non-slaves and slaves from plantations. Depending on who owned the coal field and so on whether they were slaves or non-slaves.

Extracting turpentine from pine trees and making tar is where North Carolina got its name from (the Tar Heel State).

Some Africans as time went on owned their own land and many Africa Americans worked with Africa Americans. About 12 million African people came to the New World during slavery time.

Some slaves were treated badly depending on their plantation master. Some were beaten and tied with chains to mostly make an example of them so that the other slaves would do their work and follow orders. Some of them at night escaped and ran away and found ways to slip through to the Underground Railroad to what the passage way was named. If they could succeed to get to the Northern States they were free.

Some never made it, they were caught and beaten and killed at the hands of the plantation owners.

Civil War:

The North won the Civil War because they had more people, more factories, and more wealth. It was an Industrial Revolution in the North. The North could build and make things faster than the South. The South put up a good fight for being less financially able to make guns, cannons, and wagons to fight a war with.

After the Civil War President Lincoln freed the slaves, many of them stayed on the plantations and worked for wages. Many slaves left the plantations and worked for a lot of free enterprise companies. Many non-slave citizens helped the slaves that left the plantations.

The slaves were citizens and treated with respect and the plantation owners could not harm them, if they did they could be fined or locked up in jail. The free slaves were to be treated like humans and had as much rights as the plantation owners did. The free slaves could start their own families and lived together as families.

Gradually this went on and it wasn't long before the State opened up schools for the free slaves that were not slaves any more could get a free education. These people were Americans and they could go to school. With some education they could get better jobs. In the late 1800's and 1900's million of African Americans left the South and migrated North where they could find better paying jobs.

Memories of the Civil War:

When the Civil War started in April 12, 1861 and ended April 9, 1865, William was 23 years of age. My grandfather was a small man approximately 5'4" tall, but was as strong as an ox. They were living in the little town of Smith, NC in Duplin County. It was not too far from the Cumberland County line and not too far from Fayetteville, NC. Before and during the Civil War the Confederate Army was recruiting every able body man young or old that they could find to enlist in the war. Some joined the army, many had to be drafted, and some were deserters.

People in the neighborhood told William that being a small man if he went to war that he would not last long. William's family did not want him to go and William did not want to leave his family.

There were not many able bodied men now in the area when the war started. William and his father Abraham Alvin were just about the only men folks in the area to keep the farm going, planting crops, and raising hogs. They also helped their neighbors, mostly women folks to help on their farms and harvest the crops. During this time, there were no roads, mostly wagons trails and old stagecoach roads.

**Figure 70 The Author's maternal grandparents,
William Billy Carter and Laura Bedford Carter.**

(William a Deserter) – (Civil War True Stories):

It wasn't long before just about every man and young man that were able to walk and shoot a gun in the surrounding area were gone.

William knew he had a big task ahead of him to keep food on the table, feed the livestock, housed the crops, and to help his neighbors.

By now William was marked as a deserter by the Confederate Army. The officers started looking for him and others in a few miles square.

This was told to me by my Grandmother Laura Carter, William's wife when I was a small child. My Grandfather William during his marriage to my Grandmother told the stories through the years about the Civil War. Again my Grandfather was 67 years of age and my Grandmother was 39 at the time they got married. William died in 1929 and Laura died in 1951. All during their marriage William told Laura about how he hid from the Confederate Army.

The whole family was on the lookout for the army officials, they did not want William to get caught. William said this is how it was. They would ride on horseback and sometimes buggies trying to find him. He had good places to hide in the woods, building, and under the house.

William knew if they came to the house at night that they would likely find him there. In the house he could not escape. To make sure that this would not happen, William and his father Abraham cut a hole in the living room floor where the dining room table was. They made a trap door where it would be easy to quickly move the table and the rug covering the hole and then be able to put the rug and table back in place quickly.

This was the year 1861 in the summer time when it was hot weather. It was told by William that this was a hotter than usual summer.

Again all this was told to me by my Grandmother Laura Carter from the time I started to school and until I was fifteen when she died November 19, 1951.

William told Laura many, many stories how it was living those few years when the Yankees came through the South.

They looked for him throughout the area. They rode through the fields and woods on horseback where a buggy couldn't go. One night the whole family was sitting on the porch and this was just about every night in the summer time. They could stay cool on the porch until the house cooled down enough for them to go to bed.

Back in those days for lights at night people had candles, oil lamps, and lanterns. This particular night everyone was sitting on the porch when two officers on horseback came around the corner of the front porch.

They did not hear them come up until it was almost too late for William to hide. This was the first time they came up to the house to look for him. They figured to sneak up to the house and they might catch him there.

William was sitting next to Zilphia who had moved in a couple years ago and was living there with Abraham. William and Zilphia were sitting almost at the other end of the porch when they saw the officers. Back then women folks wore their big long tail frocks in the summer time and winter time. Immediately Zelphia whispered to William to get between her legs and under her frock. With William being small and it being pitch dark outside, it took them a few minutes to light their lanterns. They asked had they seen William or knew where he was. Abraham told them that he left home and was going away to escape going to war.

Grandfather told my Grandmother they came up on the porch and went all through the house with their lanterns. William said that he was really scared when they searched all through the house. William said that it being dark that cloudy night and no moon out might have saved him from getting caught.

In those days during the summer the mosquitoes were bad and if you had any kind of light burning this would make things worse

"From 50,000 years ago up until now according to records there has be an estimate of more than 107 billion people or humans have lived on earth and mosquitoes-borne illness have killed more than half of the population of humans and other animals."

When the officers came out of the house, William told my Grandmother Laura Carter that if they found those deserters in the area they would put them on the front line when the battles started. William was listening to all of this still hid under Zilphia's frock and between her legs.

The following year William told Laura they came back in February 1962 looking for him. They were also looking for a few more deserters in the area.

This time it was late on this particular night. The officers thought being late they would catch him in the house. This time they came by horses and buggy. The family heard the buggy coming down the path. They saw their lanterns hanging on each side of the buggy.

Real quick they removed the table and rug and William went through the hole and down under the house. Quickly they replaced everything back as it was.

Zilphia met them at the front door and told them that William was not there, but they went all through the house a second time.

Just think about this, if they had caught him this would have changed things and it could have changed the Carter's history of a lot of the Carter families.

I mentioned before that William and Laura got married August 3, 1904 in Wayne County. He died in 1929 and Laura died in 1951. For 22 years later my grandmother told a lot of things that William witnessed during the time that Sherman came through the South.

One thing that he told Laura that stood out really good with me is when Laura told us that when our Grandpa saw the Yankees marching through the area going North from Atlanta. This was in the counties near Fayetteville, NC, Duplin Sampson, and Cumberland County

William told Laura that after the last time they looked for him in the house that was the last time. He said all during the war he was careful where he went and mostly hid in the wagons when they traveled anywhere.

Sherman's Army:

When Sherman's Union Army came through the South, they would take anything that was not nailed down. They would have to hide things or put them underground. William told Laura the Yankee Soldiers would take hogs, chickens, mules, horses, cows, goats, cured meat from the smokehouse, and anything that they could eat. William told her that Sherman's Army was a big Army. Sherman had over a thousand wagons with 6 mules pulling each wagon and men marching beside the wagons from the front line all the way back to the last wagon. They would travel six to eight miles a day. Several hundred yards across Sherman's Army had over 60,000 troops and over 50,000 mules.

The wagons would be hauling food medical supplies, grain, fodder, water, lots of clothing material, and other things that the Army needed. They would have ammunition, rifles, wagons, and several hundred cannons. Everything moved at a slow pace. Almost every soldier had to walk. William, my

Grandfather, said due to poor dirt roads and paths it took a long time before they got out of sight, just about all day.

He said they would not go far out of their way to take your things. If you got in their way or was a threat to them they would shoot you or burn your house down.

General Joseph Johnston:

Gen. Johnston was commander of the Confederate forces when the Union Army commanded by William Tecumsch Sherman's Army came through the Carolinas.

Sherman's Army marched north from Atlanta, GA into the Carolinas and when they reached Fayetteville, North Carolina the Army stopped. They made Fayetteville their command post for a few days.

During this time going north is when my Grandfather witnessed how huge Gen. Sherman's Army really was. This was in the spring, around March of 1865. By this time my Grandfather was not afraid as much as he was at the beginning of the war when they were looking for him and a few other deserters.

Several Divisions of the Confederate Army dug in at the Bentonville area waiting for Sherman's Army to get there. They knew the Sherman Army was heading in to Goldsboro to receive more supplies for his troops because lots of them had no shoes or uniform clothing to wear. All this was supposed to be a surprise attack on Sherman. But due to a cloudy dark night Sherman's Army knew by the scouts that

Sherman had sent out. Sherman's Army slipped in during the night and were well equipped to do much battle to the Confederate Army at Bentonville.

The Battle of Bentonville, NC:

On March 19 – 21 of 1865 both armies were dug in pretty good near the little town of Four Oaks, NC.

Sherman's Army out-numbered the Rebel's Army forces three to one. The Union forces threatened to cut off the only line of defeat on the second day of fighting.

Gen. Johnston knew that now was their only chance to withdraw. All of them would be slaughter if they did not slip away this night. He withdrew his army north, far away from the battle ground. The next morning it was known by the Union Army that Gen. Johnson's Army had disappeared during the night and this was a big surprise to them.

Many casualties and wounded soldiers were left on the battlefield. The John Harper's huge house was set up for the wounded and dying men on both sides of the battle. This was only a short distant from the battlefield. It accounted for 1,577 casualties all totaled with 360 buried in a mass grave next to the Harper House Family Cemetery. The rest were buried on the battlefield where most of them had died.

General Johnston's Army had lost: 2,606 total (239 were killed, 1,694 were wounded, and 673 were missing or captured).

General Sherman's Army had lost: 1,527 total (194 were killed, 1,112 were wounded, and 221 were missing or captured).

After the battle Sherman's Army marched on toward Goldsboro, NC and north to Richmond, VA.

My Grandfather witnessed the local people cleaning up the big mess at the battleground with several wagon teams hauling away everything left behind from the battle. He told Laura it took a long time before everything got back to the way it was and for the community to get over the battle scare.

After the Battle of Bentonville, Gen. Johnston sent a message to Gen. Lee saying that Gen. Sherman's Army was too big. I can do no more than annoy him, so a month later Gen. Johnston surrendered his army to Gen. Sherman. Gen. Sherman continued on his march through North Carolina and on into Richmond, VA.

On April 9, 1865, shortly after the Battle of Bentonville, Gen. Robert Edward Lee surrendered to the Union Forces.

After Lee's surrender it took about two weeks before Gen. Sherman and Gen. Johnston to get together and finalized the surrender of Johnston's Army.

On April 26, 1865, the surrender of General Joseph E. Johnston's Confederate Army to General William T. Sherman's Union Army was at the Bennett Place in Durham, NC.

There have been hundreds of books written about the Civil War; before the war, during the war, and after the war and how it affected everybody's lives for many years after the war.

As long as it has been since the Civil War, it is almost unbelievable that I had a relative, my Grandfather, William Billy Carter, that witnessed part of history and lived to tell my Grandmother Laura bout it.

Abraham and wife Mary Cox Carter:

Our Carter family started way back in the 1700's with all the records that can be found.

Abraham Carter lived from 1755 – 1817. Mary Cox Carter lived from 1764 – 1825. Both lived on a plantation in Duplin County, North Carolina near a little town of Smith, not too far from Turkey.

They became husband and wife on June 18, 1784. They were parents to my Great Grandfather Abraham Alvin Carter.

They had six children while living on the plantation. They are:

Carl Carter lived from 1786 – 1842

Sabra Carter lived from 1788 – 1837

Nathaniel Carter lived from 1792 – 1854

Sally Carter lived from 1796 - 1863

Goodwin Carter lived from 1801 – 1859

Abraham Alvin Carter lived from 1805 – 1880

History does not tell us about Abraham and Mary Cox's past.

Abraham Alvin Carter:

Abraham Carter was born in 1805 in Duplin County, North Carolina. He had seven children with Betsy Elizabeth Carter, four children with Hester Hetty, and only one child with Julia. He died in the year 1880 in his hometown of Smith, NC, having a long life of 75 years.

Abraham Alvin Carter was the son of Abraham Carter and Mary Cox Carter. They all lived in Duplin County, NC, near a little town called the town of Smith in the center of good farming country.

Abraham Alvin Carter's First Marriage:

Abraham Alvin and Betsy Elizabeth were born the same year of 1805 on a plantation in Duplin County, NC. Abraham was born into slavery. Abraham was an African American, Betsy was a white woman her father owned the plantation. They lived on the plantation and they became in love with each other. They knew each other from birth.

Betsy's father did not want his daughter to marry Abraham. After many years they got married in the year 1832. They both were 27 years old. They had seven children.

Betsy Elizabeth lived from 1832 – 1896

Susan lived from 1836 – 1918

William lived from 1837 – 1929 (My grandfather)

Louisa lived from 1847 – 1850

Jesselived from 1838 - ????

James lived from 1843 - ????

Alex lived from 1848 – 1850

It was not uncommon for a man to have two wives living in the same household in the early years.

In the year 1843, Abraham Alvin married Hester Hetty, an African American. After five years of living with both wives, in the year 1848, Betsy died with complications from child birth with Alex Alexander and Alex only lived 2 years after birth.

Abraham Alvin Carter's Second Marriage:

In the year 1843, Abraham married Hester Hetty. Hester was an African American, she was born in 1824. Abraham was 19 years older than Hester. Hester died in the year 1858 after giving birth to Susan. She died in Duplin County, NC.

Abraham was 38 years old when he and Hester Hetty became husband and wife. They had four children, one son and three daughters. William Billy Carter was six years old when they got married.

Will Carter was born in the year 1843

Rheraby was born in the year 1853

Elizas was born in the year 1855

Susan was born in the year 1858

Back in those days there was no way to travel fast. The fastest travel back then was by horseback, a buggy, or a stagecoach. Even then there were no doctors nearby. There was no way to save a baby, its mother if the mother had complications having a child, one of both could die.

Abraham's Family:

In the year 1858, when Hester died, William Billy Carter was 21 years old. His father Abraham Alvin was 54 years old. By now there were twelve people living with Abraham: Elizabeth, James, Susan, Alberta, Will, Cherry, Pheraby, Elizar, Susan's daughter Susan, Jesse, Allafrah, and William.

A year after Hester passed away an African American woman by the name of Zilphia Zilphy came to live with Abraham.

The Carter family has records of her living with them. There are no records in history who she was or where she came from. There are no records of her and Abraham being married.

My Grandfather William Billy Carter told my Grandmother Laura Bedford Carter that Zilphia was younger than Alvin Carter. Lots of people called Abraham "Alvin" back then.

Again my Grandmother Laura died in 1951. She died 21 years later. She told us when we were little about William's life, living in the old days. She had many, many true stories that William told her.

After Zilphia moved in, it did not take long for some of the children to not like her, especially Will. After a few months and getting more acquainted with the family there were more children she did not like and they did not like her.

Will was half-brother to William. Will was about 16 years old at that time.

It was told that Zilphia would make up lies on some of them misbehaving and when Abraham came home from work at night he would use his belt on them with the lies that Zilphia made up.

Will was in particular the one she did not like. William had a job with a local milking company in Turkey, Duplin County, NC. One morning shortly after William went to work, Will came by with his clothes in a big bag under his arms. He told William that he did not want to live there anymore because of his stepmother, "that is what they called her" Zelphia.

William told Will that Abraham would miss him badly because Will would not be there to help with the farming and look after the livestock. Will told William that he was mad and did not care what happened. He said he was leaving and would not come back and would be too scared to come back home. He left walking down the road toward

South Carolina. It was told that Will ended up in Georgia and went to work on a hog farm in Georgia. That was the last that they knew about Will.

Abraham Alvin's Third Marriage:

Years after the Civil War, history does not tell us what happened to Zelphia Zilphy. Some said that she went back to her people. William said that she was a middle aged woman a little younger than his father, Abraham Alvin Carter.

William lived with his father until he got married. Abraham was 70 years of age when Zilphia left. Most of Abraham's family was living with him, along with several grandchildren.

Abraham and Julia got married in February 8, 1874. Julia was an African American. She was born in the year 1835. She was 39 when she and Abraham got married. She had one child born in late 1874. They named her Victoria Carter. Julia died a few weeks after the birth of Victoria with complications from her birth.

Julia had lived about one year with Abraham. Abraham died in the year 1880 at the age of 75. Victoria was six years old. The records prove that this is correct.

William married Dorothy "Dollie" Susan Kornigay the same month and year that his father Abraham married Julia.

My Mother's Big Families:

On the Carter side my mother, Nance Carter Woodard, had a big family of Uncles, Aunts, brothers, and sister. On the Bedford side she had even a larger family of half-brothers, sisters, nieces, nephews, Uncles, and Aunts.

History of my mother Nancy's mother Laura Bedford Carter:

Laura's father was John Thomas Bedford, born September 17, 1848 and died April 10, 1925 at the age of 76.

His father was Counsel Bedford born in the year 1820 and his mother was Delilah Harris born in the year1825.

Laura's mother was Catherine Katie Grant born February 14, 1852 and died September 26, 1880 at the young age of 28.

John and Catherine were married on November 19, 1868. John was 20 and Catherine was 16 years old. This was John Bedford's first marriage.

They had five children within their 12 years of marriage before Catherine died. Their names are:

Laura (my grandmother) - born October 2, 1869 – died November 16, 1951

Charlie Columbus Bedford – born September 2, 1876 – died July 25, 1933

Lucy D. Bedford Gay – born October 5, 1873 – died June 25, 1954

Jeanette K. Bedford Forehand - born November 12, 1875 – died November 30, 1974 at the age of 99

John C. Bedford – born November 24, 1876 – died September 11, 1918

Laura was 81 years of age at death

Charlie was 64 years of age at death

Lucy was 81 years of age at death

Jeanette was 99 years of age at death

John was 42 years of age at death

John Thomas Bedford:

Laura's father was John Thomas Bedford and her step-mother was Caroline Dixie Pike (born May 4, 1866 and died December 26, 1930 at the age of 64).

John and Dixie were married on August 28, 1881. Dixie was only 15 years old and John was the age of 33. Caroline had her first child at the age of 16 and her last at the age of 41. At this time John was 60 years of age.

John and Dixie had thirteen children and they were Laura Carter Bedford's half brothers and sisters. Dixie did good to have lived for 64 years having that many children because back then there were not many doctors available, only mid-wives or your next door neighbor.

Their children were:

James Bedford born December 4, 1882 – died June 3, 1889, he only lived six years.

Patience W. born January 20, 1883 – died February 9, 1912 at the age of 29

Dora Hiddabelle born September 10, 1885–died November 7, 1971 at the age of 86

Ruth Naomi born October 2, 1889 – died December 29, 1964 at the age of 75

Frank Lester born December 13, 1891 – died December 17, 1969 at the age of 77

Nance Nannie born August 2, 1894 – died October 19, 1921 at the age of 27

Kline D. born December 8, 1897 – died February 6, 1931 at the age of 34

George D. born August 17, 1897 – died July 30, 1914 at the age of 17

Jack born in 1901 – died November 10, 1929 at the age of 28

Joseph Stanley born January 4, 1903 – died April 10, 1976 at the age of 73

Emmett Orvin born September 15, 1905 – died September 17, 1981 at the age of 76

William Jennings Bryon born August 26, 1907 – died July 27, 1980 at the age of 72

Jack Bedford born in 1901 – died December 16, 1929

Jack committed suicide at the age of 28 on November 8, 1929. He had one child, a daughter with wife Laura Fields. She was 3 years old. Jack and Laura were married February 22, 1920, their daughter Dorothy Helm was born November 26, 1926. Jack shot himself with a shot gun in the left chest. Again this was my grandmother, Laura Bedford's half-brother.

William Billy Carter's First Marriage:

My grandfather was 36 years of age when he married Dorthy "Dollie" Susan Kornegay on February 10, 1874. Dollie was born May 4, 1854. She was 20 when they got married.

Dollie was the daughter of Issac Kornegay and Kathy Duncan Kornegay from the little town of Smith, Duplin County, NC. They had six children.

They were:

Ann E. "Annie" Carter lived from 1875 – 1938

Frances "Frannie" Carter lived from 1878- 1933

Governor Zeb Vance Carter lived from 1881 – 1968

Pickney C. Carter lived from 1882 – 1967

Martha Sudie Carter lived from 1885 – 1957

John Gordan "J.G." Carter lived from 1892 – 1917

They lived in a little town of Turkey near Smith, NC, in Duplin County.

William was employed with a big hog farmer. He worked hard and lots of hours breeding sows, mixing up feed mixture for the little pigs, and keeping everything repaired. With several hog pollards, while the little pigs were being born sometimes William had to stay overnight if a sow might have her litter of pigs during the night. Most of the time, he could tell if a sow was about to have her pigs. It is the action of the sow about how long it will be before she gave birth to her litter of pigs.

William, my grandfather, had to watch out for the little pigs while being born so that the sow (Mother hog) did not lay on them. This was important because for every pig lost, this would be money lost. William was about 49 years old at this time in history, his wife Dollie was 33. It was told that Dollie was a beautiful woman.

Their children were small, this was the year 1887. Their oldest child was Annie Carter she was eleven at this time.

Most of the time, his boss, the owner of the hog farm would check on William from time to time. If he needed help he would help him with the sows giving birth and other things that were needed on a hog farm, such as mixing up feed for the hogs and see that they had plenty of water.

William had not seen him this day and it was getting dark. He needed help with the sows and pigs because this night was unusual because the sows were birthy pigs more than usual. When a sow birthed a litter of pigs it is best for some-one to be there and keep the sow from laying on them.

He needed help immediately and the only person he had was Dollie. He only lived a short distant. He walked as fast as he could to get her to help him. She had done this before if he needed help with the hogs.

When he arrived at his house he confronted his boss at the house. He and his boss had a big dispute, why was he there and he did not go to the hog farm.

After the episode of what took place that night at William's house, a friend of William's came over that lived nearby. He told William that even with his rights that his boss was well liked in the community and that he had a lot of kinfolk and friends. He need to leave that night and if he waited until the next day some of his friends could kill him.

William and his wife Dollie loaded everything they could in a two horse wagon and left that night with their chil-dren. William had some friends in the Pikeville area near Goldsboro, NC.

This trip was about 45 miles to travel from Turkey, Duplin County to Wayne County to the little town of Pikeville. They traveled all throughout the night by oil lanterns and most of the next day. His friends welcomed him, Dollie, and their children.

William and Dollie lived with them for a short while. It did not take long for them to find a house nearby. William never heard anything from Turkey in Duplin County after he left.

About what happened between William and his boss has lingered on in the locals minds for years and years. Some old timers still remember the episode of what happened.

William's Jobs:

William worked as a laborer with Mr. Bedford. This is how he met Laura Bedford, my grandmother. Mr. Bedford was Laura's Uncle. A few years later Dollie died at the age of 38 on September 8, 1891. They were married for 18 years.

William was 54 years of age when Dollie passed away. He still lived in the Pikeville area working with Mr. Bedford. At this time, William's older children were working to help support the family.

William worked other jobs at times when Mr. Bedford did not need him. Every so often William would see Laura Bedford. As time went on, William and Laura became friends. They would see each other working on the farm. Everybody knew that William was a good worker and he was good to his and Dollie's children. William and Laura were becoming really good friends and began seeing more of each other.

By this time William's children had grown up. The older ones had left, got married, and off on their own, except for the younger ones.

My grandmother, Laura Bedford Carter was a hard working woman. What times she was not working in the fields she helped women in their homes doing things such as quilting blankets, cleaning houses, and she did a lot of work in her garden. William and Laura continued on seeing each other.

William Carter and Dollie's Children and their Family:

<u>**First Child:**</u>

Ann E. "Annie" Carter born November 8, 1875. She died May 6, 1938 at the age of 62. Annie married Thomas Lane on April 24, 1896. Thomas was born February 10, 1870 and died December 4, 1938.

They had four children:

> Willie Lane born in 1897 and died in 1913
>
> Ernest Lane born in 1898 and died in 1966
>
> Nannie Mae Buck Lane Bradley born in 1906 and died in 1970
>
> Charlie Lane born in 1911 and died in 1954

Annie and Thomas were buried in the Patetown Cemetery, Patetown, NC in Wayne County.

<u>**Second Child:**</u>

Frances Fannie" Carter Carter was born on October 9, 1878. She died April 28, 1933 at the age of 55.

France married Abraham "Abram" Carter in the year 1898. I have no name of Abram's father or mother. They could have been second cousins. Abram was born November 15, 1873 and died October 2, 1944 at the age of 70.

Frances and Abram had four children:

>Lillie was born August 1898 and died in 1910 at the age of 12

>Bettie Dolby was born November 27, 1903 and died January 27, 1964 at the age of 61

>Clarence was born April 3, 1904 and died October 24, 1965 at the age of 60

>Edgar was born in 1908 and died in 1920 at the age of 12

Third Child:

Governor Vance Carter was born February 10, 1881 and died March 11, 1968 at the age of 87. Vance married Julia Frances Lee who was born February 10, 1892 and died June 24, 1971 at the age of 79.

They had eight Children:

>Zeke Dee Carter born October 6, 1910 and died October 28, 1951

>at the age of 41

>Zeno Carter born December 17, 1912 and died July 11, 1978

at the age of 66

Annie Mae Belle Carter born February 7, 1915 died January 8, 1969

at the age of 53

William Henry Carter born September 24, 1917 died March 8, 2008

at the age of 91

Sonnie Carter born June 1, 1920 died May 29, 1983

at the age of 63

Marvin Nathan born September 4, 1921 and died August 24, 1999

at the age of 78

Carrie Elizabeth born November 9, 1924 and died November 25, 2000

at the age of 76

Floyd Daniel born January 25, 1927 and died November 4, 1990

at the age of 63

Fourth Child:

Pinkney "Pink" C. Carter was born June 26, 1882 and died January 15, 1967 at the age of 84.

He married Mollie Polly L. Dora Pate on May 5, 1906. Mollie was born April 8, 1889 and died October 12, 1985 at the age of 96.

Pink and Mollie had nine children:

James Allen Cater born May 14, 1907 and died September 16, 1988

at the age of 81

Archie Floyd Carter born September 27, 1909 and died March 20, 1965

at the age of 55

Elizabeth Carter born July 8, 1912 and died January 12, 1975

at the age of 63

Lizzie Carter born in 1913 – no other records

Leonard Hayes Carter born October 6, 1914 and died May 18, 1991

at the age of 76

Raymond Jarvis Carter born February 13, 1917 and died February 17, 1963

at the age of 46

Essie Pauline Carter born July 6, 1921 and died January 1, 1989

at the age of 67

Letha Mae Frances Carter born January 31, 1924 and died December 25, 1998 at the age of 74

Sidney L. Roy Carter born August 29, 1926 and died February 19, 2016 at the age of 89. He married Josephine Anderson on August 22, 1946. They had no children. Josephine was born February 25, 1927 and died August 10, 2006 at the age of 79

Fifth Child:

Martha Sudie Carter Sykes was born on January 31, 1885. She died August 7, 1957 in Goldsboro, NC in Wayne County at the age of 72.

Sudie was married two times:

Her first marriage was at the age of 16. She married George Dickerson on December 22, 1910. He was a black man at the age of 23. They were married in Independent City near Dorrville, VA.

George was born November 9, 1885 and died February 28, 1972 at the age of 86. He died in a little town near Donville, VA called Gretna, VA. He was buried in the Fairview Baptist Church Cemetery at Gretna, VA. Sudie and George were only married three years, they had no children.

Sudie's second marriage was to James Henry Sykes. They were married on November 25, 1906 in Wayne County, NC. James was 19 years old and Sudie was 20. James was born September 1, 1886 and died July 19, 1949 at the age of 62.

James and Sudie had four children:

A. Dollie Mae Sykes

B. Jerry Sykes

C. Respers Tarp Sykes

D. Luther Odell "Tom" Sykes

A. Dollie Mae Sykes was born August 3, 1907 and died February 10, 1987 at the age of 80. Dollie married Oscar Barnes at the age of 16 and Oscar was 20. Oscar was born September 6, 1902 and died July 22, 1990 at the age of 86.

Oscar and Dollie had two children:

Oscar Barnes Jr. born in 1930 and died in 1951

Ollie Ray Barnes born in 1939 and died in 2018

B. Jerry Sykes was born on May 22, 1909 and died August 30, 1993 at the age of 84. Jerry married Lola Medlin, born April 22, 1913 and died April 10, 2000 at the age of 86. Jerry was 22 and Lola was 18 when they got married in the year 1931.

Jerry and Lola had two sons:

Raymond Randolph Sykes born in 1931 and died in 1998

Ray Junior Sykes born in 1948 and died in 1999

Hazel Carter married Raymond Randolph Sykes. Raymond's grandmother was Martha Sudie Carter Sykes, Hazel's half first cousin. Martha Sudie Carter was Hazel's father Charlie Carter's half sister. William Billy Carter was Charlie Carter and Martha Carter's father by two marriages.

C. Respers Tarp Sykes was born September 1, 1917 and died August 29, 1982 at the age of 65. He married Ida Ophelia Benson. She was born August 4, 1918 and died July 16, 1999 at the age of 80. They were married on October 9, 1937. She was 19 and Respers was 20.

Respers and Ida had five children:

Peggy Elizabeth Sykes born in194- and died in 1980

John Respers Sykes born in 1944 and died in 2013

George Ray (Hot Rod) Sykes born in 1948 and died in 1999

They have two children living at this time. No record on them.

D. Luther "Tom" Odell Sykes was born on August 2, 1922 and died March 14, 1986 at the age of 63. Tom was married four times.

His first wife was Hattie Elizabeth Langston born in 1922 and died June 8, 1940 at the age of 18. Tom and Hattie were married on October 21, 1939. Tom was 18 and Hattie was 17. Hattie died June 8, 1940 at the age of 18 after 9 months of marriage. Her death certificate is not legible enough to read. There were no children.

Tom's second marriage was to Martha Mae Potter, born in 1914 and died in 1993 at the age of 79. Tom and Martha were married June 28, 1941.

Tom and Martha had one son:

> Ray Sykes born September 24, 1948 and died in 1999

No records on how long they were married.

Tom's third wife was Blanche Elizabeth Anderson. She was born January 1, 1927 and died November 29, 1966 at the age of 39. They were married on October 24, 1959. Blanche was 32 and Tom was 37 when they got married. Tom and Blanche were married for 7 years.

Blanche died because her clothes caught on fire. She lived for three weeks with third degree burns and the lack of blood flow throughout her body.

Tom's fourth wife was Carolyn Anne Benson. Anne was born June 10, 1944 and died September 1, 1991 at the age of 47. Tom and Anne were married about 1968. Anne was 24 and Tom was about 46. No records could be found. They had no children.

Tom was married four times and had no children.

Sixth Child:

John Gordon Carter was born on December 14, 1892 and died September 5, 1917 at the age of 24. He married Lillian "Lilly" Daubigny on January 4, 1915 at the age of 22 years.

Lily was born on March 8, 1883 and died November 21, 1962 at the age of 79 in Wake County, Raleigh, NC. John and Lilly were only married less than two years when John died.

John and Lilly had two children:

Majorie Ethel Carter

Raymond Crumwell Carter

Marjorie Ethel Carter was born on March 5, 1916 and she died on December 25, 2004 at the age of 88. Ethel married Jefferson Thomas Cavenaugh who was born on June 6, 1913 and died on July 26, 1989 at the age of 75. They were buried in Elmwood Cemetery in Fremont in Wayne County, NC.

Marjorie and Jefferson had five daughters:

Mamie Cavenaugh was born in 1908 and died in 1985

Bernie Cavenaugh was born in 1911 and died in 1935

Pearl Cavenaugh was born in 1916 and died in 2002

Lucille Cavenaugh was born in 1920 and died in 2006

Mary Magdalene Cavenaugh was born in 1922 and died in 1996

All were of Wayne County, NC

Raymond Crumwell Carter was born on March 8, 1917 and died on September 7, 1949 at the age of 32. Raymond married Rosa Addie Pitman. She was born on October 9, 1916 and died on April 13, 1961 at the age of 44.

They were married on September 9, 1939 in Wayne County, NC. They were both 22 years old at marriage.

Raymond and Rosa had five children:

> Kenneth Carter was born in 1936 and died in 2005 at the age of 69.

> There are four children still living all from Wayne County, NC.

Raymond and Rosa are buried in Elmwood Cemetery, in Fremont, NC

William's Second Marriage:

On August 3, 1904, William and Laura Bedford became husband and wife in Pikeville, NC in Wayne County. William was 67 years old and Laura was 39.

Laura had a child by the name of Katie. Katie was five years old when they got married. William was the son of Abraham Alvin Carter and Betsy Elizabeth Carter. William was a Mulatto person because Betsy was a white woman.

William and Laura had four children:

> John William Don Carter was born in 1905 and died in 2003

> Charles Andrew Carter was born in 1908 and died in 1980

Nancy Carter was born in 1910 and died in 1969

Bessie Carter was born in 1911 and died in 1911

Bessie lived 5 months.

William was born on September 8, 1837 and died in Wayne County on June 9, 1929, he was 92 years old.

Laura was born on October 2, 1869 and died November 10, 1951 at the age of 81.

William and Laura' oldest son was John William Don Carter was born on December 9, 1905 and died on April 8, 2003 at the age of 97. His wife Lillie Florence Thomas was born on June 12, 1907 and died on November 13, 1997 at the age of 90. They were married for 67 years. They got married on December 16, 1924 in Kenly, NC.

Don and Lillie had four children:

William Franklin Bill Carter – "deceased"

Margie Lee Turner of Wilson, NC

Kathy Overton of Kansas City, MO

Nell White of Savannah, GA

Don and Lillie were married on December 16, 1924. Don was 19 years of age and Lillie was 18. They were buried in Selma Memorial Garden.

Their son William was buried in the Bedford Family Cemetery in Pikeville, Wayne County, NC. His wife Elizabeth H. Carter is still living as of this writing.

History does not tell me about the three daughters, because they are still living.

Charlie Andrew Carter was born October 25, 1908 and died June 29, 1980 at the age of 71. He married Lannie Blackman. She was born on April 30, 1913 and died on February 15, 1959 at the age of 45. They were married on January 10, 1931, he was 22 and she was 17. Charlie and Lannie were married for 29 years.

Charlie and Lannie had three children:

Edward Carter was born on June 5, 1933

Hazel Carter was born on September 7, 1935

Mary Helen Carter was born on March 19, 1941 and died on February 4, 2015 at the age of 73.

Edward married Velma Rose on September 19, 1952. Edward Carter is 86 years old and Velma Carter is 87 years old. Both are still living. They have no children.

Charlie's Second Marriage:

Charlie married Ida Jane Braswell Rowe. They were married in the 1960's and were married for 21 years.

Charlie and Lannie are buried in the Bedford Cemetery in Pikeville, NC in Wayne County.

Ida Jane Braswell Rowe Carter is buried with her first husband Albert Clarence Rowe in the Cemetery at Fellowship Church near Princeton, NC.

Hazel Carter was born on September 7, 1935. She married Raymond Randolph Sykes sometime in 1951 at the age of 16, Raymond was 20.

Raymond was born on May 14, 1931 and died on February 20, 1998 at the age of 66. Hazel and Raymond were married for 43 years.

Raymond and Hazel have two children:

Albert Wayne Sykes was born on March 21, 1956. He married Jacqulynn Dawn Eason on July 31, 1975.

Vickie Diane Sykes was born on December 24, 1959. She married Wilbert Daniel Evans, Jr. n May 16, 1981.

Raymond is buried in Selma Memorial Gardens, in Selma, NC. Hazel is still living at the age of 83.

Mary Helen Carter was born n March 19, 1941 and died on February 4, 2015 at the age of 73.

Mary's first marriage was to Oscar Jessie Medlin. He was born on August 29,1918 and died February 22, 1998 at the age of 80. They were married on June 19, 1960. She as 19 and he was 41. They were married about 5 years. They had no children.

Mary's second husband was William Avery Hamilton. He was born October 12, 1935 and died April 19, 2013 at the age of 77. Mary and William were married in the year 1966. They were married for approximately 47 years.

Mary and William had one son:

Jody Wayne Hamilton was born on July 29, 1967 and died in 1980.

Jody died by drowning in the Neuse River in Smithfield, NC at the age of 12 or 13. Jody was Mary Helen's only child.

Linwood Ballard Woodard:

My Father, Linwood Ballard Woodard was born on April 9, 1903 and died on November 13, 1983 at the age of 80. His father was Charles Thomas Woodard and his mother was Nancy Ellen Woodard. Both were Woodard – "no kin".

Ballard had three brothers and three sisters:

Alton V. Woodard was born in 1906 and died in 1991

William Tommie Woodard was born in 1909 and died in 1989

Willie Albert Woodard was born in 1916 and died in 2002

Agne Woodard was born in 1908 and died in 1983

Fannie Rosetta Woodard was born in 1912 and died in 1999

Sallie Mildred Woodard was born in 1917 and died in 1993

Ballard married Nance Carter Woodard, my mother. They were married on April 21, 1929. My father was 26 and my mother was 19. My mother was born on February 6, 1910 and died on March 21, 1969 at the age of 59.

My mother gave birth to six babies:

#1 Her first child was Lenwood Ballard Woodard, Jr. He was born on February 16, 1930 and died on March 5, 1997. We called him L.B. He was a special needs child, but he lived to be 67 years old. He was buried in the family cemetery near Princeton or Boone Hill, Johnston County, NC.

#2 birth of baby sister, Dorthy. She was born on November 17, 1931 and died on November 27, 1931, she lived for 10 days. She was buried in a home-made coffin and was buried in the family cemetery.

#3 Roy McCary Woodard was born on November 18, 1932 and died on September 12, 1992 at the age of 59 with colon cancer.

Roy's first marriage was to Virgina Edwards on January 3, 1952, he was 19 and she was 18. They were married for 13 years. They had no children. Roy and Virginia divorced on August 23, 1965.

Roy's second marriage was to Patsy Akins. They were married on July 23, 1966. Patsy had two daughters, Dona and Teresa.

Roy died in Durham Regional Hospital on September 12, 1992 in Durham County. He was buried in Durham County at Woodlawn Memorial Port Cemetery.

They were married for 22 years. Roy and Patsy had no children of their own.

#4 Sister Laura Ellen Woodard was born on December 3, 1933. She is living at the age of 85. She married Willard Fernie Bill Edwards on September 9, 1950. He was 21 and she was 16.

Bill was born on August 25, 1929 and died on September 21, 1998 at the age of 69. Bill died with a cerebral hemorrhage. He lived a few hours after getting help for himself. Bill was buried in the Kenly, NC Cemetery in Johnston County, NC. Bill and Laura were married for 47 years. Bill's parents were Levie and Leafy Edwards.

Bill and Laura had three children:

> **Fernie Eugene Edwards** was born on February 18, 1953. He died in 1955 with cancer cells. He was buried in the Kenly Cemetery.

> **Ronnie Joe Edwards** was born on November 4, 1955 and died on March 29, 1983 at the age of 27. Ronnie was never married. He died with an Epilepsy seizure and fell in water behind his mother and father's house in Nahunta and drowned.

Ronnie was a good well liked young man, not only did he work hard with his job in Goldsboro NC he helped with their big bird farm near Nahunta.

Ronnie was looking after the birds and feeding them when he had his seizure and fell in a small place of water. He drowned before he could recover from the seizure.

Eugene and Ronnie's sister Billie Jean Edwards is still living. She is married to John Wesley Carter. They were married on June 8, 1986 at the family home near Nahunta. There was a big turn-out for the wedding.

John and Billie Jean have two sons:

Wesley Matthew Carter

Ronnie McCray Carter

Fifth Child: Father and Mother Ballard and Nancy Woodard:

#5 Merlon Patrick Woodard was born on December 2, 1935. Merlon is the author of this book.

#6 Sixth child: Baby Boy Woodard was born on June 9, 1937 and died on June 9, 1937. He died because of a difficult birth. Most mothers back in the early years had their babies at home with a mid-wife of someone that has helped mothers before. But due to my Mom's condition and being so big, they decided to have the doctor out of Boon Hill to deliver the baby. They got the doctor in time and he drove out on his old Model T Ford.

When he got there Mom was in labor and he did his best to deliver Baby Boy. At this time in the early 1900's they did not take the baby by C Section or Cesarean Section. This came about in the 1920s but only in some hospitals. After World War II in the 40's more babies were being born in the hospitals and only a few were born at home.

The doctor did all he could. He told my Father that his wife was too small to have a baby of this size. I was told when I was born Mom had a difficult time giving birth to me because I weighed 7 pounds 1 ounce at birth.

The doctor told my Father he could only save the Mother or the child. He told dad with the 4 small children that he and my mom had it would be best to save their mother. I mentioned in my book earlier about mothers having babies at home.

The only way that the doctor could save my mom was to kill the healthy baby boy and save my mother from dying.

My baby brother weighed in at 10 pounds on the doctor's scales.

The death certificate read that baby boy died from a difficult birth due to cerebral injury to his brain. His head was just too big.

Merlon Patrick Woodard (Father):

#5 **Merlon Patrick Woodard** married Tommie Oastine Pulley on February 4, 1956. Merlon was 20 and Tommie was 18 at the time of marriage.

Tommie was the daughter of Herman Pulley and Pauline. She had a brother Travis and sister Sandra.

Merlon and Tommie divorced on September 12, 1979 after 22 years of marriage.

Merlon and Tommie had three children:

> #1. Reginald Myron Woodard was born on July 10, 1957
>
> #2 Brian Patrick Woodard was born on February 13, 1962
>
> #3 Tammy Lynn Woodard was born on October 19, 1966

#1 **Reggie** worked all his adult life at Duke Medical Center and most of his years, 32 years with Wake Hospital in the Administration Department.

Reggie retired this year (2019) from Wake Medical. Reggie is 62 years old today, July 10, 2019.

He has a good retirement and he will live around the water or ocean and in the mountain area in the states of NC and VA. Reggie is not married and has never been married.

#2 **Brian Patrick Woodard** has had several small jobs while in high school and out of school and at the age of 21, Brian joined the Navy Seabees (CB) Construction Battalion.

He married June Lusby on June 13, 1983, he was 22 and June was 19. They divorced in the year 1996 after 13 years of marriage.

Brian's second marriage was with Mary Ellen Cowart on September 10, 1999. They were divorced on April 1, 2008 after 9 years of marriage.

Brian joined the navy Seabees (CB) at the age of 21 on May 16, 1982. The Seabees (CB) is the Construction Battalion of the Navy Force. He came out of the Navy after five years on May 3, 1987.

Brian then joined the Rocky Mount Police Department in June of 1987. After three years with the Rocky Mount Police Department he missed the Navy and joined back up with them in November of 1990. He kept his rank and continued on from there.

The CB is known as the US Navy Construction Battalion better known as the Seabees. Their job in the Navy is to build hospitals, airports, runways, military barracks, warehouses, mess halls, and they are trained to fight. They are sharpshooters. Their main jobs are to pave the way for the Marines and report to that branch of service what is going on. They pick up all the information they can and report back to the Marines so when the fighting begins the Marines will know and be better prepared.

During war time or not they will sneak into areas to explore. They are taught to fight and sneak out. It takes a special breed of a person to become a CB.

All total Brian was in the CB's for a total of thirteen years and this was during the conflict with Iraq. They played a big part in that war. His home port was Gulf Port Mississippi from there he went to Rotor Spain to build a hospital, an air port, runways, barracks, and mess halls for future Seabees.

They went to Guam and built a hospital, warehouse, barracks, and mess hall there. They did a lot of repairs to things that were already there.

Brian and June had two sons:

> Brian Patrick Woodard, Jr. was born on December 13, 1985. He is 33 years old now. He has a supervisor position of heavy equipment in building bridges.

> Their second son Merlon Shane Woodard was born on January 6, 1991 and died on December 18, 2005 at the age of 14 due to an accident.

When Mary Ellen and Brian were married, Mary had a son at the age of six. His name is Jonathan Cowart, he is now about 27 years of age.

Brian became a nurse in 2004. This is his current job now doing Home Health Care Services in the homes for the dying and handicap children and adults.

Jonathan Cowart went to college in Florida to study Marine Life of different species of marine life such as the manatees and other mammals in the ocean. He is highly educated on this subject.

#3 **Tammy Lynn Woodard** was born on October 19, 1966 in Pitt County in Greenville, NC. She married Eric Batchelor.

Tammy and Eric had one son:

Patrick Thomas Batchelor was born on November 21, 1987 and died on May 23, 1999 at the age of 11 years.

The cause of Patrick's death was Batten Disease, a fatal disease of the nervous system of the brain causing the brain to produce less neurons. This is a bad gene the child gets from both parents with the same gene.

The progressing loss of function of neurons which is similar to Alzheimer, causing the cells to die and will always be fatal.

A child is born with this disease and show signs from about 4 to 10 years of age. They begin to lose their hearing, become blind, can't walk, or feed themselves. It is so rare that there are only 3 cases out of ten hundred thousand births.

It will lead to death within 2 to 4 years if the child is taken care of really good, if not the child will die quick. Both parents have to have this genetic gene for a child to have Batten Disease. Even though both parents can have this same gene, some of their children can be born without the Batten Disease. Sometimes all their children can have the disease and not one would be free of it.

Tammy's second marriage was on June 1, 1989 to Haywood Eugene Hallowell, They divorced on July 24, 2001 after 12 years of marriage. They had no children.

Tammy Hallowell and Shaka Peykamian began living together in the year 2002. Due to diplomatic reasons they have not gotten married.

They have a son:

Darrin Thomas Peykamian was born on December 13, 2001, He is 17 at this time.

He will soon be out of high school and will start to college after high school. He has a good job while going to school. Darrin will graduate in 2020.

Tammy has two jobs at this time. She is employed with the Garner, NC Physicians and Wake Medical Center in Raleigh, NC. Her positions are in the medical records and discussing things with patients' Insurance Companies and the doctors. This is a tough job.

I hope this book has inspired the younger generation that nothing is free you have to make your own way. You have to decide what you want out of life and which way you want to go to become somebody or to be a dead beat all your life. No one will ever hand you anything. If you are not careful the dishonest people will swindle you out of what you got. The way life is now you have to be smart and have good common sense to know the difference. Yes, you can be somebody but it is all entirely up to you. The hard working people are the ones that have made our Nation what it is today. You have to count your blessings every day. What God has given you is you life and it's all in your hands. Now and with God's help you can have your dream and contribute a lot to society. You must follow your dreams and don't be a quitter. Yes you can do it. Don't have an impossible dream, make the better of it and let that dream become reality. In the end of an old age you will look back and say that I am somebody and I fought a big fight but I accomplished my dreams.

"The Author"